Lawyers

Professional Ethics and Court Etiquette

*Foreword by the Hon. Michael Kirby AC CMG,
Former Justice, High Court of Australia*

OAGILE BETHUEL KEY DINGAKE

INDIA · SINGAPORE · MALAYSIA

Notion Press

Old No. 38, New No. 6
McNichols Road, Chetpet
Chennai - 600 031

First Published by Notion Press 2020
Copyright © Oagile Bethuel Key Dingake 2020
All Rights Reserved.

ISBN 978-1-64828-867-8

This book has been published with all efforts taken to make the material error-free after the consent of the author. However, the author and the publisher do not assume and hereby disclaim any liability to any party for any loss, damage, or disruption caused by errors or omissions, whether such errors or omissions result from negligence, accident, or any other cause.

While every effort has been made to avoid any mistake or omission, this publication is being sold on the condition and understanding that neither the author nor the publishers or printers would be liable in any manner to any person by reason of any mistake or omission in this publication or for any action taken or omitted to be taken or advice rendered or accepted on the basis of this work. For any defect in printing or binding the publishers will be liable only to replace the defective copy by another copy of this work then available.

DEDICATION

To my family

I owe everything I am able to do to their never failing love and support.

CONTENTS

Acknowledgements   *7*
Foreword   *9*
Preface   *11*

1. Introduction   15
2. Qualities of a Good Lawyer   19
3. Lawyering Skills   26
4. A Lawyer's Duty to the Court   32
5. Civility and Integrity-Core of the Profession   38
6. Etiquette   46
7. Independence   55
8. Dress Code for Lawyers   64
9. Honesty, Integrity and Fairness   68
10. A Lawyer's Duty to the Client   73
11. Confidentiality   77
12. Conflict of Interest   81
13. Diligence   85
14. Professional Negligence   89
15. Preparing and Presenting Evidence in Court   95
16. The art of Cross-Examination   107
17. Lawyer's Fees   115
18. Discipline   118
19. Conclusion   121

References   *131*

ACKNOWLEDGEMENTS

This publication would not have been possible without the input of a number of colleagues in Botswana and Papua New Guinea. I thank in particular Justice Harold Ruhukya who edited this manuscript. I also wish to thank my revered brother, and former judge of the Australian High Court, Hon Michael Kirby AC CMG for graciously agreeing to pen the foreword to this book. Of course, as is the norm, I should indicate that any mistakes herein are mine and mine alone.

FOREWORD

The legal profession guards its reputation and utility by requiring lawyers to abide by rules of professional conduct & etiquette. Ethics are central to legal practice. A profession's most valuable asset is the extent to which the public has confidence in it. The sad truth, however, is that, across many jurisdictions, the public appears to be losing faith in the ability of the legal profession to uphold the highest ethical standards, competence, integrity, independence, honesty and fidelity to the law.

In recent years across the Globe, the legal profession has seen many instances of deterioration in standards. Some lawyers do not adequately communicate with their clients. Some fail to give timely updates of progress of their matters. Other fail to avoid, or to notify, conflict of interests and duty. Many fall behind in updating their legal knowledge. Unfortunately, some lawyers, a small minority, are guilty of misappropriation of their client's funds or property.

A lawyer should not engage in conduct which is dishonest or unbecoming or that which may cast doubt on that lawyer's integrity as a fit and proper person to practise law. A lawyer must at all times avoid compromising professional integrity or independence. Each one of us bears a personal responsibility for good behaviour. How individuals conduct themselves reflects on the profession as a whole.

In representing a client, a lawyer must follow all lawful instructions given by the client. Once a lawyer has accepted representation of a client, he or she must advance the case of the client without fear or favour. As an expert, a lawyer must not hesitate to advise a client that a case carries low prospects of success, if that be the lawyer's considered opinion.

With these basic rules, explained at the outset by Judge Dingake, I am certain that this book will help lawyers recommit themselves to adherence to the highest standards of ethical conduct and etiquette. Law is a profession. Lawyers are under a duty to observe civility and professionalism in the course of litigation and in their everyday interaction with each other. The law often needs reform and updating. The work is often stressful. We must not be blind to its defects. But it is the duty of all of us to hand on our profession to future generation with an even higher reputation than in the past.

I am grateful to Judge Dingake for inviting me to write a foreword to this book. I commend it to lawyers cross the Globe. From the perspective of his experience, Judge Dingake offers good advice and wisdom for us all.

The Hon. Michael Kirby AC CMG
Former Justice, High Court of Australia
Sydney NSW 2000

PREFACE

Every lawyer, as an officer of the court should be a champion of justice, and proud to be a worthy player in upholding, and deepening the basic precepts of the rule of law and an independent judiciary. The rule of law and an independent judiciary are not possible without an ethical legal profession.

Across the world there is concern that ethical standards of lawyers are declining, despite many jurisdictions having rules of professional conduct and etiquette in place. This publication is a humble attempt to promote adherence to the highest ethical standards of the legal profession. The publication is not intended to be an exhaustive treatise of the subject, but it is hoped it may assist particularly those newly admitted, in better understanding their ethical professional obligations. I also discuss related topics such as professional negligence arising out of any breach of duty a lawyer owes to a client and the all-important attributes of a trial lawyer being cross examination and preparing witnesses for trial.

Given the above, one cannot talk of an independent judiciary without an independent legal profession whose purpose is to speak with knowledge and authority on matters of law and justice, particularly with respect to the protection of fundamental human rights and freedoms.

It is hoped that the discussion of lawyer's professional ethical obligations will assist lawyers in representing clients more effectively and upholding the principles of integrity, honesty, fairness and justice that are intrinsic to the legal profession and the administration of justice.

The judges and the legal profession have a shared commitment to the realization of the highest commitment to ethical standards at all times. We are both committed to a legal system that inspires confidence among the public. Judges are trained lawyers and in this publication whenever I use the term: "we" I am referring to lawyers generally, including judges.

Lawyers must be trustworthy and independent. An independent lawyer is an integral part of a credible and independent administration of justice. The lawyer's first duty is to the court and thereafter his client. This balance must always be kept in mind.

The lawyer's professional standing is a matter of the Law Society, the professional body of which he is a member and obliged to obey its standards and rules of conduct. Where his duty to the court conflicts with his duty to his client, the duty to the court takes precedence. The lawyer who misses this point may not be a fit and proper person to practice law.

Every lawyer has a duty to promote and defend the interests his client. In doing so he should not be cowed into submission by any authority, not even a judge. His duty is to raise every issue, advance every argument and ask every question, however uncomfortable which he thinks will help his client's case. But, as an officer of the court concerned in the administration of justice, he has an overriding duty to the court. It is his duty that when he argues in court, he must not lend himself to casting aspersions on the other party or witnesses for which there is no sufficient basis.

A lawyer must not withhold authorities or documents which may be against his client but which the law or the standards of his profession require him to produce. He must not accuse his opponent of fraud when there is no evidence to prove such a serious allegation. He must be courteous and respectful to all the participants in the court process, such as the judge, his opponents and witnesses.

Lawyers should argue against each other with respect and under no circumstances should they allow themselves to be carried away by the emotions of the client's case.

A lawyer's duty to the court arises out of the practitioner's special relationship with the court; it overrides the duties owed by a practitioner to clients or others. The lawyer's duty to the court includes candour, honesty and fairness. Public confidence in the administration of justice depends on the honesty and reliability of a lawyer and his respect of the administration of justice. The duty of candour and fairness is critical to the lawyer's role as officer of the court. It is no excuse for a lawyer who breaches his primary duty to the court to argue that he didn't know or that he was recently admitted as a lawyer.

Preface

It is therefore important that a lawyer should do nothing that would obstruct the administration of justice by: deceiving the court; withholding information or documents that are required to be disclosed or produced under the rules concerned with discovery, subpoenas; abuse the process of the court by preparing or arguing unmeritorious applications; wasting the court's time by irrelevant arguments; coaching clients or their witnesses as to the evidence they should give.

Additionally, the lawyer owes a duty to the court to inform it of legal authorities that bear one way or the other upon matters being litigated upon. The duty applies irrespective of whether or not the particular authority may be unfavourable or not. It is normal for lawyers to draw the judge's attention to any adverse authority and then seek to show how that case is different from the one currently serving before the judge.

Through strict adherence to the highest ethical standards lawyers can help in ensuring that the legal profession is trusted by the public and continues to be regarded as an " honourable" and " noble" profession.

CHAPTER ONE

INTRODUCTION

Ethical standards comprise of principles and duties that lawyers owe to the Court, their fellow lawyers and clients. These standards are not necessarily the same, although the goal may be the same. Legal ethics are necessarily contextual and subjective. It is defined in large part by the legal culture, and the broader environment of which lawyers are part. What is ethical for a lawyer in the United Kingdom may not be considered ethical for a lawyer in Botswana for example.

Michael Karnavas, writes in his publication, *"Lawyer's Ethics"* that he was surprised to realise that lawyers across jurisdictions differ on whether it is proper or not to prepare a witness for trial, saying an Australian lawyer he spoke to thought it would be unethical to prepare a client for trial, a Canadian lawyer saying it would be illegal; and an American lawyer saying not to prepare a witness for a trial would amount to malpractice. This simply goes to underscore the point made earlier that a lawyer's ethics may differ from one jurisdiction to another.

In the adversarial system such as we have in Botswana, and most of the Commonwealth, the objective of a trial is to discover the truth. Bearing this consideration in mind, to prepare a witness for a trial is acceptable, as long as the lawyer does not suggest answers to the witness. For a lawyer to suggest answers to a witness would go against the objective of discovering the truth. I discuss the matter of preparing a client to lead evidence in a trial in some detail later in this book.

The importance of ethics to the legal profession cannot be over emphasized. The legal profession is rooted in old traditions based on notions of courtesy, honesty, good faith, integrity, justice and fairness that must be upheld at all times. Over time the legal profession has seen a steady decline in observing established traditions of professional ethics that evolved over centuries. The decline in standards is noticeable in Court every day in the manner in which lawyers address the Court or each other.

When I went to Law school in 1984, our ethics professor never got tired to teach us that the legal profession is a noble profession that should be characterized by honour, honesty and integrity. Ordinarily lawyers should be trusted by the public. However, sometimes you get the clear impression that the public considers them conmen and women. This is a heavy indictment and stain on the profession. The fact of the matter is that in many jurisdictions lawyers are less trusted by the public particularly when one reads horrendous accounts of lawyers misappropriating their clients hard earned money.

Lawyers (including prosecutors) although often caught up in divided loyalties as a result of their duty to the court and clients, must at all times remain committed to justice and fairness. It is inevitable that these duties will be in conflict. In cases where the lawyer's duty to the client and the court conflict, the lawyer is obliged to fulfil his or her obligations to the court. This is not generally understood by clients, or by some lawyers who carry the notion of the duty to the client too far and engage in practices that are unethical and that go to defeat the interests of justice. Examples would be an allegation of fraud against other lawyers in circumstances where there is no evidence to support the claim; deliberately delaying proceedings in order to force a settlement from the opposing client who is concerned about increasing costs or gaining some tactical advantage.

Ethics is central to the practice of law. It is rooted in the values of justice, fairness and equity. If lawyers do not adhere and promote these ethical values then the law will fall into disrepute and people will resort to alternative means of resolving conflict.

It would be dangerous and unhealthy for any society for people to lose faith in the law on account of unethical conduct of lawyers. It is true that a profession's most valuable asset is its collective reputation and the confidence bestowed upon it by the public.

Conclusion

This chapter sought to sketch in broad strokes the primary obligations of a lawyer as a service provider; to underscore the importance of ethical conduct and competence. A lawyer must also remember he is hired as an expert and that if his conduct falls below that expected of him by his peers he may be liable if his incompetence causes injury or loss. A lawyer must be his client first judge and be able to advise of the prospects of his client's case succeeding in court; and if it is a completely hopeless case he is at liberty to decline to represent the client. At that stage the client is of course entitled to consult another lawyer.

CHAPTER TWO

QUALITIES OF A GOOD LAWYER

There are certain general qualities that a good Lawyer must have. A number of them come with experience and a few can be picked from books. Below I discuss the ones that I consider important without following any order of priority.

Courage

Lawyers need lots of courage as more often than not what they stand for may not be in the interest of another person or even the majority. In pursuit of justice courage is of critical importance. What then is courage? It is the state of mind that is resolute and fearless – and in the context of the law, resolute and fearless in achieving justice. Courage is the power to face and overcome danger, fear and injustice. People consult lawyers not only for their expertise but also their courage as defined.

Nelson Mandela said that courage is not the absence of fear but the ability to manage fear. That may well be so. Courage is about endurance usually fuelled by wisdom and considerations of justice. During Mandela's days at the height of apartheid in South Africa, both as a lawyer and a politician, courage may have meant taking up causes or options that may result in death, but you took them all the same because you believe it is worth doing so far the common good of humanity. In life, however, hardship is normally transient. It is also true that in life a person may either survive current challenging circumstances or not. The key is to overcome fear, in the course of preparing for a better future.

Wisdom is an important fuel for courage as it invariably dictates that it is the right thing for any person to pursue a just cause. At the end of the day a courageous person becomes content and fulfilled and more successful in his profession because he can be trusted and driven in the position he adopts.

Good Communication Skills

A lawyer must have a good command of the language of the court and be able to communicate well orally and in writing. In order to argue convincingly in the courtroom before a judge, good public speaking skills are essential. Communication and speaking skills can be developed during the period of study by taking part in activities such as mooting courts and general public speaking. Lawyers must also be able to write clearly, persuasively and concisely. Being clear, brief and to the point is an important skill to possess.

Analytical Skills & Sound Judgment

All lawyers should be able to take instructions from client and analyse the evidence from all possible angles. They must be able to identify the strengths and weaknesses of a case, if they are to render any helpful meaningful advice. Lawyers are called upon whenever instructed by client to use their expertise to arrive at a judgment that is sound having regard to the facts presented to them and the applicable law. They must be able to identify the strengths and weaknesses of their client's case and that of the opponent and advise the client accordingly. It follows therefore that sound judgment is an important trait for a good lawyer.

People Skills

Law is not an abstract practice. At the end of the day lawyers work with people, on behalf of people, and are often instructed to challenge decisions made by people that affect other people. It follows in my view that they must have people skills; be personable and persuasive and be able to read even body language. It is these people skills that allows them to decide upon the best approach to take in order to achieve the desired outcome.

Negotiation Skills

These days lawyers are encouraged to settle matters out of court if it is possible to do so. This requires ability to negotiate and reach a better deal for your client or at the very least achieve a win - win situation beneficial to some extent to both parties. There are many cases in which viewed broadly it is not necessary to litigate even if the client has a good case. This is because litigation, other than being expensive, may take time and be emotionally draining. A good lawyer, who has good negotiation skills would seek to leave all parties feeling like a reasonable outcome was achieved rather than trying to run over the opposition.

Compassion

The fact that lawyers work with people to resolve their issues requires that they be compassionate. Compassion is an emotional attribute whereby one perceives another's problem and authentically and sincerely wants to help resolve the problem. This is part of what lawyers do every day. Clients consult lawyers to resolve their legal problems and naturally expect to receive an empathetic hearing.

A compassionate lawyer focuses on how others feel and is accepting of their perspective, whether or not he ultimately agrees with it. Without compassion, you cannot put yourself in your client's shoes to fully understand the issues your client faces. Without compassion, it is difficult to understand your adversary's position, anticipate what they may do and be able to take pre-emptive steps to benefit your client. Without compassion the lawyer lacks the necessary ingredient to be driven to achieve the best result for the client.

Ability to Listen

The ability to listen is important virtue. Many people hardly listen, they just give the impression that they are listening. One of the important aspects of communication is listening. It is difficult to communicate effectively if you can hardly remember what your client was saying or what the counter argument to your client's case is. Lawyers we are required to analyse and synthesize instructions given, and exercise good judgment and advice client accordingly. To do so effectively we must be good listeners. We must be able to understand the version of our clients and that of the opponent.

Assertiveness

A lawyer needs to be assertive. Being assertive does not translate into being disagreeable or aggressive. Being assertive is the ability to state your case clearly and firmly while remaining respectful of others. Aggressive lawyers often unjustifiably attack others. It is not a good trait at all and does not engender proper debate.

Quite often aggressive lawyers cannot understand the other party's. That makes them ineffective at understanding the problem they have been entrusted to resolve. Aggressive lawyers tend to be rude and toxic. Obviously this kind of behaviour is more likely to damage any sense of collegiality. An A aggressive approach tends to shut out reasoning and the end result is failure to resolve an issue, often at great cost to the client.

Creativity and Perseverance

Lawyers often say that every case turns on its own circumstances. Indeed in the real world no two cases are necessarily identical requiring identical treatment.

In law whilst precedent is important, it should not act to kill or suppress creativity. Sometime the justice of the case may require that old precedent be revisited and if need be overturned. Sometime lawyers must apply their minds to new ways of approaching a matter and not be stuck in the stone-age way of doing things.

While in private practice my law practice was characterized by some creativity that generated interesting jurisprudence. I once took up a point in the Industrial Court, in Botswana, that the Court cannot compel workers who had embarked on unlawful strike to go back to work because to do so would amount to forced labour that is prohibited by the Constitution.

I had not realised when I raised the point that the Constitution actually prohibited forced labour "save when it is ordered by a Court". When this was brought to my attention by the C court, I had to be creative, and think fast on my feet, I then argued that the Industrial was not a "Court" as contemplated by the Constitution.

I argued that this was so because the judges of the Industrial Court are not chosen through the mechanism of the Judicial Services Commission (JSC), but by a Minister and that the court is also constituted by lay persons, making it a tribunal, but not a court. The court thought I had raised a weighty point and discharged the order ordering workers to report to work and referred the matter to the High Court to determine whether the Industrial Court was a 'Court' or a tribunal. The point is that by sheer creativity on my feet I delivered a positive result for my clients.

Perseverance is also an important trait for a lawyer. We must always persevere in pursuing a cause we believe to be just. We should never take short cuts. We must be thorough in our preparation. Our pleadings and submissions must be of high quality. We must not give up easily and where we think a matter is arguable, we should be able to take it to the apex court.

CHAPTER THREE
LAWYERING SKILLS

The preceding chapter discussed the broad qualities and attributes of a good lawyer. In this chapter I discuss more specifically some important skills lawyers must have, if there are to be effective in their trade. Lawyers are, more often than not hired to advance the case of their clients in court. Their skills as lawyers come into play immediately after instructions. Their listening and abilities to process facts and apply the law are immediately implicated in a trial situation in particular. If he agrees to progress the client's matter he may need to communicate with other persons involved in the matter and, if need be, ultimately draft pleadings.

In court once the matter is ripe for argument his voice is critical as he has to be heard clearly by the court as he seeks to persuade it in one way or the other. To this extent a lawyer's voice is an important asset; and so are his mannerisms. Book knowledge in and of itself can never teach anyone to be a good lawyer. Nothing, in my considered view, beats plain old experience. The techniques of lawyering vary from person to person. However some skills such as preparing well for a case can be learned, or at least discovered objectively.

Lawyering involves the ability to argue a case competently in court by the correct application of the law to the facts. In jurisdictions such as Botswana where the bar is fused attorneys are also advocates in the sense that they are not confined to just interacting with clients but are also permitted to argue cases in court. In some jurisdictions the bar is divided between solicitors and barristers. Solicitors consult clients and prepare briefs for barristers who would in turn argue the matter on the basis of such briefs in court.

In this chapter, wherever the term advocate/barrister is used, it means a lawyer who has the authority to argue a case in Court. The art of lawyering is in part one of communication and one of persuasion – persuading the Court of the applicable law to particular facts of the case.

There are a number of qualities essential to effective lawyering, *viz*, good voice, good command of the language of the court, confidence, persistence, practical judgment and experience. I discuss these attributes briefly below:

Voice

A clear, distinct voice is an asset. It is gold. It carries the essential message to the Court. It is important that the Court must understand what your arguments are and the basis of those arguments. A good command of the language of the Court is important. It can invigorate the debates and clear ambiguity that stands in the way of advancing a client's case. A measured and audible voice is important, as are variation of pitch and tone. The loud monotone may be understood, but it loses the attention of the Court easily. In order not to lose judges' attention who most of the time would be taking notes, it is good not to be too fast and if the judges are busy writing, watching their pens may be a good guide as to the speed with which to address the Court.

Confidence

Confidence is extremely important. It conveys the message that the lawyer knows what he is talking about and is not a chance taker. Confidence usually comes with experience and knowledge of the procedural and substantive law. Confidence enables a lawyer to make a good case to the end in spite of unexpected difficulties. Confidence is usually accompanied by persistence. Persistence is not the same thing as being unreasonable or being difficult. Experience teaches that cases may be lost but they should not be abandoned, and the courage to persist in a difficult cause is important.

Strategy and Tactics

Strategy is the art of preparation of a case, based on a clear understanding of the strengths and weakness of the case and that of your opponent. A good strategist who has "a smoking gun" does not waste the Court' time, he puts his best argument upfront at the earliest opportunity. For instance, if you are the defendant and the plaintiff has no standing; it may be important to take up that point first and bring the case to an end fast instead advancing other arguments that may be weak and bring up the strongest point towards the end. Similarly, it is equally important to abandon a point that initially appeared strong but in the course of argument is proven unsustainable.

A good lawyer must be able to vary or modify an argument in the course of arguments. To stubbornly refuse to adjust when it is necessary to do so may have adverse reputational consequences.

Preparation

As indicated earlier, to succeed in any case one needs sound preparation based on detailed knowledge and understanding of the law. After the pleadings are closed, there is nothing better than a properly prepared and conducted case, ascertaining the law and the facts. The evidence proposed must be the best evidence available. It must contain all facts, all exhibits and any explanation that a Court properly directing itself may wish to be clarified.

It is also useful to explain to witnesses, experienced or not, how to give evidence – not what they should say, but the mechanics of giving evidence. Essentially, you should ensure that the witnesses understand the following: (a) where to go, where to stand and where to find the Court; (b) how to address the judge; (c) that their answers to questions are the evidence. By way of illustration a good practice would be to explain to the witness that: "If you do not hear the question, ask to have it repeated. If you do not understand the question, say so, do not guess at the answer. Your answer is the evidence – if you guess wrongly you may be thought to be lying or unwilling to assist the court determine the matter".

It is also useful to distinguish for the witnesses the difference between examination-in chief and cross-examination and to instruct them to answer questions as asked. A good lawyer does their best to prepare their witness not to answer more than is asked or, as oft happens, not to offer explanations for their answers unless specifically asked to do so. The precepts are: (1) The shortest truthful answer is best. Do not add anything or volunteer anything to the cross-examiner. (2) Listen to his questions and answer that question. There is nothing wrong in advising the witness that if he can give a completely truthful answer by stating "yes" or "no" or "I don't know" or "I don't remember" that should be the answer to give.

Where a witness is likely to come under a strong attack from the cross-examiner it is best for him to realize this in advance. An astute lawyer should safeguard the case he is being called to support, and where possible, shield the witness from unpleasant shocks and surprises.

In my experience in a trial, evidence is primary, the law secondary. Once the facts are known the law is often easy to ascertain and apply.

Tactics

Tactics is essentially the ability to think on one's feet. The ability to do so varies from one individual to another. As with most aspects of lawyering experience is the best teacher. You can offset lack of experience by application and preparation. Preparation is key to facilitating tactical thinking. If you do not allow yourself to be diverted from your chosen line of attack, and have looked at both the strengths and more particularly the weaknesses of your case, you will in all likelihood survive the most difficult phase of a trial.

Necessary in understanding the subject of tactics is mastering objections. These present a tactical difficulty, whether with respect to evidence on affidavit or being given by a witness under oath or to questions inadmissible in form. Lawyers must choose when to object with extreme care. Any objection must be substantive and warranted. Lawyers may object against inadmissible evidence, not admissible evidence that is simply against them or their client. As a general rule unnecessary objections should be avoided. Sometimes objecting to harmless leading questions is time wasting and may well be counter-productive. Lawyers should not suggest answers to witnesses and need not be reminded by the Court that it is wrong to lead a witness. Sometimes there is very little doubt that prompt objection must be made; but at other times the decision can be very difficult as to when to make it.

Pleadings are the foundation of every case. They drive evidence. Leading evidence that is not pleaded is a waste of time and should be avoided. Evidence must be marshalled according to the pleadings.

CHAPTER FOUR

A LAWYER'S DUTY TO THE COURT

The first duty of lawyer is to the court and secondly to the client. Where a lawyer's duty to the court conflicts with his duty to his client, the duty to the court is the paramount consideration. As officer of the court concerned with the proper administration of justice a lawyer has an overriding duty to the court.

Every lawyer has a duty to his client to fearlessly raise every issue, advance every argument and ask every question, however uncomfortable which he thinks will help his client's case. But, as an officer of the court concerned with the proper administration of justice, he has an overriding duty to the Court, to the standards of the profession, and to the public, which often conflicts with his client's wishes or with what the client thinks are his personal interests.

A Lawyer must not mislead the Court. He must not lend himself to casting aspersions on the other party or witnesses for which there is no sufficient basis in the information in his possession. He must not withhold authorities or documents which may be against his client's but which the law on the standards of his profession require him to produce.

A peculiar feature of a lawyer's responsibility, reflective of his duty to the court is that he may be required him to act in a variety of ways to the possible disadvantage of his client even if the client gives instructions to the contrary. The professional ideal is not the pursuit of wealth but public service. That is the vital difference between professionalism and commercialism.

A client – and perhaps the public – may sometimes think that the primary duty of a lawyer in adversary proceedings is to secure a judgment in favour of the client. That is not so.

A lawyer must do what they can to ensure that the law is applied correctly to the case. An allegation of fraud with no factual basis 'constitutes a serious dereliction of duty and misconduct by counsel' and that the obligation not to mislead the court or cast unjustifiable aspersions on any part of the proceedings or witness arises as part of the duty to the court.

A Prosecutor's Duty

At common law a prosecutor (generally also referred to as "The State" in a criminal trial) is required to disclose all relevant evidence to an accused person, and that failure to do so may, in some circumstances, require the quashing of a guilty verdict. On sentence the State may make submissions as to sentence fairly and in an even-handed manner, and that the State does not, as an adversary, press the sentencing court for a heavy sentence. The State has a duty to the court to assist it in the task of passing sentence by an adequate presentation of the facts, by an appropriate reference to any special principles of sentencing which might reasonably be thought to be relevant to the case in hand.

Duty to act professionally with scrupulous fairness and integrity

The public interest is in ensuring that the administration of justice is not subverted or distorted by dishonest, obstructive or inefficient practices. The essence of the duties is a requirement for lawyers, (within the context of the adversarial system) to act professionally with scrupulous fairness and integrity and to aid the court in promoting the cause of justice.

In the Council of the *Queensland Law Society Inc. V Wright* [2001] QCA 58 McMurdo P (with whom Davis AJ and Helman J agreed) said:

A Lawyer's duty to the court arises out of the practitioner's special relationship with the court; it overrides the duties owed by a practitioner to clients or others. As earlier indicated the lawyer's duty to the court includes candour, honesty and fairness."

Improper to Prosecute a hopeless case

No lawyer should lend his assistance to a litigant if he is satisfied that the initiation or further prosecution of a claim is *mala fide* or for an ulterior purpose or, to put it more broadly, if the proceedings would be, or have become, an abuse of the process of the court or unjustifiably oppressive.

Not to undertake case beyond Lawyer's competence

There is an obligation on a lawyer not to take on a case as an advocate in circumstances where the lawyer is plainly unqualified for the complexity of the task or has an inadequate knowledge of the area of law concerned.

Duty to corporate with each other

Lawyers in any litigation are under a duty to co-operate with the court by making sure the trial flows easily. This they may do so by arranging any pleadings or documents serving before the court chronologically; being brief and filing proper pleadings, which define the issues and places the judge in a position to draw his own conclusions about the merits when he hears the case. It is the duty of every lawyer to assist the judge by simplification and concentration and not to advance a multitude of ingenious arguments in the hope that one of the many arguments will win the day.

It is unfair and against public policy to waste a judge's time with unmeritorious arguments. It is the duty of the advisers of the parties to assist the judge in carrying out his duty. Litigants are not entitled to the uncontrolled use of a trial judge's time. Other litigants await their turn. Increasingly judges are now putting time lines to arguments in order to achieve efficiency and avoid long winded arguments that serve no purpose.

Litigants are only entitled to so much of the judge's time as is necessary for the proper determination of the relevant issues. The lawyer's duty to the administration of justice is assisting the Court to reach a proper verdict in a prompt and efficient manner. Without this assistance from lawyers, the courts are unlikely to succeed in their endeavour to administer justice in a timely and efficient manner.

Taking advantage of a mistake by another practitioner

Lawyers must litigate in good faith. In the course of drafting pleadings or making submissions mistakes do take place. Lawyers should not be too eager to take advantage of another's mistake.

The Lawyers duty of candour

In the performance of his duties, it is the duty of a lawyer to be candid with the court. In a trial two incompatible ideas are invariably involved; the contest between opposing parties for victory and the search by the court for the truth, and the inevitable conflict between these ideas give rise to very, real difficulties. A lawyer is duty bound to disclose authorities which bear one way or the other upon matters before the court. This observation is quite irrespective of whether or not the particular authority assists the party which is aware of it. To this extent it is generally accepted that it is not appropriate for the lawyer to knowingly misquote the contents of a judgment or the testimony of a witness; the arguments of the opposing counsel; or the language used in a text-book; or knowingly cite as authority a decision that has been overruled, or a statute that has been repealed; or in argument to assert as a fact that which has not been proved.

A Lawyers duty of fairness

It is an essential feature of any civilized legal system that a party should have the opportunity to test by cross-examination the truthfulness of any witness whose evidence is tendered against him. In cross examining a witness a lawyer should have in mind Sir Alexander Cockburn's admonition, that he wields the arms of the warrior and not the dagger of the assassin. The privileges necessarily accorded to cross-examining lawyers should not be abused. It is not a license to assail the character of the witness. The lawyer should not exhibit unnecessary enthusiasm for his client's case and should not over promote his client or assure him of victory. He should only be content with doing the best for his client.

Conclusion

Lawyers have a duty to ensure fair trial irrespective of which side they represent. It is unethical that a lawyer must lend his name to misleading the Court in anyway. It is his duty to pursue the cause of his client with knowledge and thus, assist in the course of finding the truth. It is the lawyers obligation to fight any injustice according to law; and to ensure that no one is above the law and no man so poor as not to be afforded the protection of the law. This is the reason lawyers often say theirs is a noble profession. Lawyers must make it so in practice.

CHAPTER FIVE

CIVILITY AND INTEGRITY-CORE OF THE PROFESSION

The legal profession is traditionally considered to be a noble profession and the lawyers refer to each other as "my learned friend". Civility, courtesy, integrity and honour lies at the heart of the profession. As the guardians of the rule of law, lawyers should embody civility, courtesy, honour and integrity in all they do. Not only do lawyers serve as representatives of their clients, they also serve public citizens and therefore have special responsibility for the quality of justice. To fulfil these roles, lawyers must take civility, courtesy, honour and integrity as their professional standard and ideal.

Civility, courtesy, honour and integrity

Civility, courtesy, honour and integrity are essentially about exhibiting good conduct in both the private and public space. Civility, honour and integrity are necessary to a profession that acts as the guardian of the rule of law, particularly so because the legal profession is in nature self-regulating. Typically, law associations have the ultimate authority over the profession. The importance of well-functioning law associations in ensuring high standards of professionalism cannot be over emphasized.

A fit and proper person

The law prescribes the criteria for admission of lawyers. Generally, in addition to being duly qualified, a lawyer has to be a "fit and proper person" to be admitted to practice law. In some jurisdictions it is a requirement that candidates petitioning the courts for admission must cite and serve both the law society and the Office of the Attorney General who may object to the admission of a petitioner on the basis that the candidate is not a fit and proper person to be admitted to practice law. This may be the case where a candidate or petitioner has a record of dishonesty or even criminality. All this is intended to ensure that those admitted to practice have key attributes alluded to earlier, being civility, honour, honesty and integrity.

The general eligibility requirements under a "fit and proper" test, may not be easily unpacked, but at the heart they communicate the idea of conduct that is beyond reproach. It is in the interest of the profession that only fit and proper persons should be admitted to practice law.

Capacity to act in a manner that engenders respect for the law and the profession – in other words, 'fit and proper' – is a requirement for receiving a practicing certificate and, in some jurisdictions, for retaining the privilege of practicing law. It follows that aspiring and practicing lawyers should always be conscious that a law degree on its own is not sufficient to practice law. It is improper for lawyers who have not been issued with practicing certificates to appear and argue any matter in court as they would not have a license to do so. In Papua New Guinea, at the beginning of each legal year, whenever lawyers appear, they would, without probing, indicate that they have a certificate to appear and tender such certificate, often an original copy. This, I consider admirable.

Notions of 'a fit and proper' person are rooted in ethical principles informing and defining the practice of law. Those principles, having evolved over the centuries to lend a higher purpose to a life in the law today, speak plainly to a lawyer's dual duties as officer of the legal system and public citizen beyond the role of representing clients. At the very top of the lawyer's code of ethics is to be fit and proper person as earlier described.

A lawyer is not just a hired gun

A lawyer's commitment is to serve both the client and the legal system. Clients may not understand these limits. Many clients are under the misconception that because they hired the lawyer, they have the power to dictate that lawyer's conduct. It falls to the lawyer to communicate to clients that he is more than a 'hired gun', but that first and foremost he is an officer of the Court. In practice, that often means refusing a client's instructions that may require the lawyer to act unethically or even unlawfully as that may, if discovered, lead to a lawyer becoming disbarred. In my experience however, it seems some lawyers have difficulty refusing client's instructions in situations involving what is plainly frivolous litigation. This may be because some lawyers may just be intent on making money at all costs.

A lawyer should never permit to be just a hired gun. He is of course entitled to withdraw if the client insists upon taking action that the lawyer considers repugnant or with which the lawyer has fundamental disagreement. It is unethical and improper for a lawyer to abuse legal procedure by frivolously bringing or defending a proceeding, or asserting or defending an issue, as such behaviour is plainly prejudicial to the administration of justice.

Although most law schools teach legal ethics in their law schools, standards of professionalism seem to be on the decline. Substantial evidence in some jurisdictions points to a decline in abiding by the 'fit and proper' test and broader ethical standards governing the legal profession. It is problematic to pin down the incidence of incivility and unprofessional conduct because law societies do not keep a record of those violations and reliable data is hard to come by. However there are countless press reports of unprofessional conduct by lawyers. Occasionally these are brought to the attention of law societies by judges. But generally, an increasing number of judges I have spoken to across the globe lament the gradual degradation of the practice of law as a noble profession to one increasingly stigmatized by increasing acts of unethical conduct. I often reprimand lawyers who would insist on being heard and to obtain an adverse order against an opponent, without serving the other side, when they know or ought to know that the matter is not urgent or otherwise not entitled to proceed.

I imagine there are many causes for the gradual degradation of standards in the practice of law. However, one that seems obvious to me is that law societies are not enforcing strict observance of codes of ethics of lawyers and sanctioning misbehaviour. Another possible cause is inexperienced lawyers who increasingly start their own law practices without adequate mentoring and guidance.

It is in my mind beneficial to lawyers, who have recently graduated, as well as the public that such new entrants should spend sufficient time attached to senior lawyers, as interns, to learn how the practice of law is done – what in other countries is called pupillage. The period of pupillage must be long enough to enable recently graduated lawyers to benefit from such attachment. The law in practice may often be different from the law in books and it is beneficial for newly graduated lawyers to watch the law live and in motion. Perhaps the time has arrived (if not arrived is quickly arriving) where lawyers intending on establishing private law firms be refused to do so unless first spending an agreed number of years attached to a senior lawyer in practice and in good standing with the law society in the jurisdiction in which such private firm is intended to be opened.

Anecdotal evidence tends to confirm that unprofessional conduct is pervasive. I have witnessed and openly reprimanded lawyers who are rude or sarcastic to each other or otherwise engage in condescending conduct, swearing, or making inappropriate interruptions. A number of lawyers I have spoken to on this subject of condescending behaviour, indicated that quite often opposing counsel strategically employ unprofessional conduct in an attempt to gain the upper hand, typically in litigation. The complained-of conduct included, for example, deliberate misrepresentation of facts, not agreeing to reasonable requests for accommodation, indiscriminate or frivolous use of pleadings. On rare occasions lawyers may collude to obtain an order that would otherwise not be warranted.

Whatever the causes, the first step towards a real remedy to unprofessional conduct is the recognition of the deeply destructive impact of such conduct on individual lawyers who engage in it, on those subjected to it, on the bar as a whole, and ultimately on the legal system. It begins with recognition that common courtesy, respect, honesty, honour and integrity must be the cornerstone of legal practice.

Aside from the most obvious reasons that lawyers should act professionally towards each other the profession requires it of them and it is just the right thing to do. A number of tangible benefits accrue from proper professional conduct in terms of reputational gain and career damage avoidance, as well as strategic advantage in a lawyer's engagement.

Judges don't like reminding lawyers to be professional and civil to each other or mediate between bickering counsels who are rude to each other. The fact of the matter is that being disrespectful to another lawyer would inevitably register in a judge's mind. In that situation, it is possible that in a border line case, the judge has a choice between ruling in favour of the client whose lawyer was civil and professional or against the client whose lawyer has been a troublemaker. We should never forget that judges are human. In other words a lawyer's conduct can and does affect the results lawyers deliver to their clients, and ultimately the success of their practices.

It is to my mind self- evident that a lawyer's reputation for professional conduct is part and parcel of his or her reputation for excellence in practice. The moral of this narration is that a lawyer who exhibits civility and professionalism is far more likely to be an effective lawyer. It is obvious that if clients evaluate their lawyers as being effective, they stay with them; if they see their lawyers as ineffective and troublesome they will go elsewhere for legal services. No client wants to lose a case because his lawyer was rude to the judge or another lawyer.

I hope this piece can encourage the legal profession to recommit to higher professional standards; more civility among lawyers; respect of the legal profession and fairness. I am certain that should lawyers uphold some of the principles outlined herein the courts system would become more efficient and the trust and confidence of the public on lawyers as officers of the courts would be enhanced.

Various stakeholders need to play their part to provide high professional standards. Lawyers' associations must enforce strict moral codes for lawyers and sanction breaches. Judges need to play their part too by reporting unbecoming behaviour to law societies. Law schools also need to strengthen their legal ethics curriculum. Civility makes the practice of law truly honourable. Professionalism of the bar is required by the society at large, not just lawyers and judges.

CHAPTER SIX
ETIQUETTE

The Encyclopaedia Britannica Dictionary defines etiquette as "the conduct or procedure required by good breeding or prescribed by authority to be observed in social or official life". Etiquette is very important to the practice of law for a number of reasons: First, for the simple reason that lawyers are part of a profession regarded as "noble". Secondly because lawyers are professionals who operate in the public space, professionalism conveys the idea that notions of honesty, civility and integrity are an inherent part of the legal profession. It underscores the fact that in law, opposing counsels are simply opponents and not enemies. The third reason is that because lawyers are admitted as officers of the court, they invariably have an obligation to serve the court and the administration of justice.

It is essentially because the legal profession is regarded as an honourable one that its members are expected to act in a manner that is honest. They should be respectful to each other even if they disagree with each other on the position of the law. In order to ensure that the profession remains honourable, it is important that lawyers abide by professional codes of conduct. Although rules are central to legal practice they tend to be disregard with impunity. I cannot over emphasize the importance of rules to legal practice. These are bright lights that guide and give direction to orderly Litigation. Court rules must be obeyed. It is good practice for lawyers to exhibit knowledge of the rules.

I must indicate that compliance with rules of court is the hall mark of a good lawyer. By rules of court I also mean rules of etiquette. A lawyer with good manners is likely to be listened to and even earn the empathy and sympathy of a judge. Lawyers or their witnesses should always show due respect to the Court and other court users. Lawyers should not unduly impugn the integrity and reputation of other lawyers or witnesses. A discourteous counsel may at the end of the day harm his or her client's cause. The rules of etiquette are part of the rules of convention that define the legal profession. They must be obeyed at all times, even if inconvenient.

The most important rule of etiquette is this: *stand up when you address the Court and bow and say "May it please the Court"*. This is a mandatory rule and must not be disregarded. In fact addressing the court whilst seated, other than being disrespectful, is contemptuous. It impugns the authority of the court. In Botswana one senior counsel was once committed for contempt, for refusing to stand even after being ordered by the court to stand and ended up being imprisoned and denied bail later that day. In denying him bail, which he had sought on urgent basis, the court said the transcript showed beyond doubt he set out to deliberately impugn the authority of the court.

It is good practice to stand not only when addressing the court but when being spoken to by the judge and throughout one's examination or cross-examination. The opposite is true. When you are not speaking or being spoken to you do not stand. If during your address your legal opponent stands to object or indicates he/she wants to object, it is good practice to yield respectfully so that the judge can conduct the trial smoothly. My experience is that some lawyers would object to the objection even before the judge hears what the objection is all about. That is not proper.

In making any objection the lawyer must use decent language. It is unethical to impute impropriety to another lawyer or cast doubt on his/her personal integrity or launch unwarranted personal attacks on an opponent.

When addressing a judge, one must maintain eye contact and listen carefully to a judge who wishes to clarify a point. The impression which your eye makes on the judge is going to be a significant factor affecting the extent to which he is prepared to listen to you. This rule applies across the board: it applies in Magistrates Courts, in the District Courts, and in the Superior Courts.

Precedence in the legal profession is very important. It also applies to judges. It is therefore good practice to allow the most senior lawyers to argue their matters first. These days this practice is dying in most courts across the Commonwealth. It needs to be revived. It adds honour and nobility to legal proceedings. Senior Lawyers who the tradition favours with the honour to go first must repay that honour by showing their juniors how to conduct themselves and how to present arguments in court.

Giving senior lawyers precedence is a mark of respect; it also brings some order and sense of purpose to court business. In that way senior lawyers are motivated to take leadership and inspire junior lawyers on the art of lawyering. It is orderly in that everybody then knows his place in the que and prevents unseemly jostling and jockeying for places, and the spectacle of senior lawyers looking lost and standing in a court packed with their juniors. The rule simply stated is this: you should always give way at the Bar table to a practitioner senior to you and give him your seat.

It is also good practice to seek permission of the court if a lawyer wants to converse with his/her opponent on any point or with a witness or wants to give a witness a document to confirm. The process of a witness confirming any document must be done transparently, and it is good practice to give one's opponent an opportunity to see the document in question. The courts would invariably allow counsel to converse with another lawyer or a witness. The courts usually proceed with caution to permit conversations between counsel and his/her witness because sometimes recording that conversation may not be easy. Usually, there is no need for a lawyer to be pacing up and down to handover documents to a witness because there is always a court orderly who is employed to do exactly that and this preserves and enhances the decorum of the court.

A lawyer should not quarrel with the judge. To do so is bad advocacy. It puts one's case in jeopardy.

Lawyers are duty bound to help the court do justice to the parties. They should not prejudice their client's cause at the expense of justice. This does not mean they should disbelieve their client unnecessarily, but if the facts are clear and unassailable, a lawyer who pushes a line that disregards common cause facts that are relevant to the case, does harm to his/her reputation as a lawyer.

In some jurisdictions, like in Botswana, it is common for lawyers to seek to see a judge in chambers before a matter commences. One may have instructions to make an application for recusal or for some other reasons. In other jurisdictions, like in Papua New Guinea, lawyers hardly see judges in chambers, and the division between the bench and the bar in that sense is much stricter. However, in jurisdictions where it is done, it is good practice, to always see the judge with your opponent in tow. More often than not no judge would see a lawyer who has a matter before him alone in his chambers. To do so only raise questions about the judge's impartiality in the matter.

It is courteous and proper to see a judge in chambers to introduce yourself if you have not appeared before the Judge in the past. It is good practice to go with your opponent.

In the same vein private communication with a judge amounts to unethical conduct. All official communication on any matter in court must be addressed to the Registrar or any properly designated officer of the court. Justice thrives better in an open and transparent environment.

In the case of *R v Brady* (Court of Criminal Appeal, 29th July, 1977, unreported, at pp.3, 4), the Court stated that:

> *"It is a deeply rooted principle that justice must not be administered behind closed doors – court proceedings must be exposed in their entirety to the cathartic glare of publicity. There are limited exceptions to the observance of this principle but these are well defined and sparingly allowed. Statutes are made by public processes. They are judicially administered in public proceedings…Moreover publicity of proceedings is one of the great bastions against the exercise of arbitrary power as well as a re-assurance that justice is administered fairly and impartially."*

There is another rule of etiquette that is equally important and should be observed at all times. This rule is that when the Judge comes into court remain standing until he has bowed and taken his seat or the proclamation to be seated has been made. This is elementary courtesy and also a rule of etiquette which must be observed.

It is worth repeating that courtesy is not only to be extended to members of the profession, that is, the judge and your fellow counsel but also to all the ancillary members of the court, such as court staff. It costs little but gains much to say thank you to the court officials who take documents to and from the witnesses, lawyers and the judge.

When a lawyer rises to address the court he must be courteous and say "*May it please the Court*". This is more than a meaningless or empty phrase or a courtesy. It opens the rest of the lawyer's day activity in court. What remains unclear to me, to date, is whether it is appropriate to start off by saying "good morning or good day My Lord/Your Honour". I am still conservative on this and prefer that lawyers must go straight to the formal introductions such as: "may it please the Court", my names are such and such and I appear in this matter for the Plaintiff".

Language and courtesy is everything to the court. To this extent it is in-appropriate to refer to a fellow lawyer by name. It should always be "my learned friend" at the commencement of addressing the court. Thereafter, it is fine to simply say "my friend". To this extent it is worth mentioning that it is not proper to refer to a litigant who is not a lawyer as "my learned friend". The phrase "my learned friend" is traditionally reserved for lawyers. Once, during my days at the bar, the late Justice Gyke Dako, formally of the High Court, reprimanded a Police Prosecutor (who was not a lawyer) referring to a defence counsel as, "my learned friend".

A lawyer should never address the judge in the second person. This means, never call a judge "You". If you wish to address a judge directly about something he has said, it is quite improper to say, "as you said a moment ago".

The correct expression or way of expressing oneself is: "as Your Honour said".

One of the essential requirements of becoming an effective lawyer, related to using appropriate language, is to know your judge. First, it is important to argue to, not with, the judge or judges. At every stage of the argument you must show respect and occasionally employ the term, "with respect". As any experienced lawyer well knows argument in court normally takes two forms – advancing a proposition in support of an application where there is no indication of the thinking of the Bench and where making the same submissions to a Bench that is clearly not persuaded and of a rapidly hardening and different opinion. Where a lawyer picks a hardening of attitude to his position he must tread carefully or perhaps conclude by suggesting, "I accept this point may well be a contentious. I leave it to your Lordship(s) to decide". Where it is clear that the judge or judges do not agree with your line of reasoning, it is discourteous and unethical to say: "I think your Lordships are wrong". Instead, try a line that may be persuasive. Sometimes like, "My Lord/Lady, I respectfully submit that the evidence on closer scrutiny bears me out, but I would not belabour the point any further.

Remember, the one cardinal rule when arguing in court is that you make submissions as opposed to expressing opinions. You do not say "it is my opinion". The court is not interested in, your private opinion as to the law or the facts. Your right is to be heard and to advance submissions of law of your client. These must be arguable. It is the duty of every lawyer representing a client to take any point which he believes to be fairly arguable on behalf of his client. A lawyer should not usurp the province of the judge. He is not to determine what shall be the effect of legal argument.

In representing his client, a lawyer is expected to plead his client's case with fearless vigour and determination. It has always been recognised that counsel has 'an overriding duty to the court, to the standards of his profession and to the public'. This overriding duty requires him to contribute to the orderly, proper and expeditious trial of causes in the courts.

Lawyers must cultivate the habit of thorough preparation. They must be ready to cite a relevant authority of a case whose circumstances are similar to the one serving before the court especially if the legal preposition urged upon the court is not common cause.

When you cite case law to any court you should do so carefully and precisely. If possible, a typed list of authorities should be available for the Court. It is good decorum before citing the case to say "might I refer Your Honour to the decision of the High Court in… which is reported in Volume … of Botswana Law Reports at page 909… It is also acceptable to say to the Court:" I refer to the judgment of your brother Dingake J and if the judge is no longer serving, to say "Dingake J as he then was".

CHAPTER SEVEN

INDEPENDENCE

The lawyer's independence is one of the core values of the legal profession. To the rule of law an independent bar is as important as an independent bench. The bar exists to provide independent legal services to clients in accordance with the law. Without an independent legal profession, it is not possible to speak of a functioning rule of law. The independence of a lawyer and the freedom of a lawyer to pursue a client's case is sacrosanct to a civilized order.

As part of the independence of lawyers, every lawyer has ethical obligations to discharge towards the client viz a viz;

- ☐ the Courts and other authorities before whom the lawyer pleads the client's cause or acts on the client's behalf;

- ☐ the legal profession in general and each member of the legal fraternity.

- ☐ the public for whom the existence of an independent bar, is an essential means of safeguarding human rights in the face of the power of the State and other interests in society.

There are three (3) aspects of the lawyer's independence:

- Independence from external influences;
- Independence from the client and professional detachment; and
- Independence from the lawyer's self-interest.

Notwithstanding the universality of the principle of independence of lawyers, it is essential to appreciate what was said earlier, namely that the nature and character of ethical obligations may differ from one jurisdiction to another.

The values of the legal profession are to do justice according to law. Every legal system, whether in civil or the common law, aims to discover the truth at a trial. Lawyers as officers of the court are a critical aspect of the machinery of justice. If they are not independent, if they are corruptible and incompetent justice would remain a pipe dream for many people. A lawyer should at all times, place the interests of his client above his own and strive to vindicate the rule of law. He must give his clients unbiased expert opinion about any matter they bring to him and once he agrees to litigate he must do so with diligence.

Independence from External Influences

The independence of a lawyer means that the lawyer must be independent of the State and other interests, and must not allow his or her independence to be compromised by improper pressure from business partners. The lawyer must also remain independent of his or her own client if the lawyer is to enjoy the trust of third parties and the courts. Consequently, on matters of law, of which the lawyer is the expert, he cannot be dictated to by the client.

A legal advice meant to please the client, and not grounded on verifiable facts and the law is unethical, inappropriate and without any value. It is indispensable for the administration of justice and the operation of the Rule of Law that a lawyer be absolutely independent in carrying out his mandate. It would be impossible for a lawyer to protect clients if he or she is subject to interference from others, "especially those in power". Reference to 'those in power' does not just mean the executive. It means other entities who may wield social, emotional, spiritual, economic and political power.

The independence of a lawyer allows him to protect his client from wrong decisions taken by the Courts. Where a lawyer believes that the Court took a wrong decision and there is still room to appeal, he must advise his client accordingly without fearing anyone. He must protect his client from violation of his rights and as long as his client gives him the mandate to proceed further, he must go so far as the apex Court if necessary.

There are many examples of how lawyers may be said to be compromising their independence. These include;

- Offering, promising or giving any commission or referral fee or a gift (apart from items of modest value) to any client, professional client or other intermediary;

- ☐ Lending money to any such client, professional client or other intermediary; or

- ☐ Accepting any money (whether as a loan or otherwise) from any client.

The independence of lawyer also precludes him from being compromised by political affiliations and family relations; in properly representing clients. Conversely, it would be similarly wrong for a lawyer to use those relations to benefit a client.

One of the most vexing questions is whether a lawyer who is a known member of a political formation can take up a case in Court that seems to go against the cause of which his political party stands.

In my mind there is no one single answer to this question. The question would depend on whether there is a conflict of interest. If there is a conflict of interest a lawyer should not take a case of a political opponent if there is a real risk that he may not perform his duties as a lawyer diligently to protect the interests of his clients. Politically, it is possible that such a lawyer may bring his political credentials into some doubt, but as lawyer he is required to be independent and fearless. The lawyer should not engage in politically expedient manoeuvring. In such cases, the duties of a lawyer must prevail over that of political interests. It is often said cynically that most lawyers who find the ethical obligations of a lawyer burdensome end up becoming full time politicians and those that are happy to comply remain full time lawyers.

Independence of government or "in-house" Lawyers

Lawyers will not only ply their trade in a law firm or, for those working for the State, from the Attorney General's chambers. There are those who would be employed as government lawyers or as "in-house" lawyers by parastatals or corporate entities. An important question, and one often times the subject of debate, is whether it can be properly said that such lawyers are independent given that in the hierarchy of the place they work they are required to report to, or are answerable to a higher officer?

In these instances, such lawyers, even though are for all intents and purposes employees of the organisations in which they work, cannot be said to exercise independence because their opinions on a matter are subject to approval of somebody else. They may advise on the position of the law (in fact that is what they were employed to do) but I would argue that their views would, at best, be opinions that must be subjected to the final approval of the governing body of the organisation such as a management committee or board of directors in terms of the vision, objectives and goals of the organisation. By signing on as employees what they do as lawyers in that organisation must have the stamp of approval of their supervisors. If they do not do as expected or directed, they would open themselves up to the possibility of disciplinary measures on many fronts. It is in those instances I would argue that they cannot exercise nor do they have independence in the strict sense. The role of government lawyers although similar in many respects to those of "in house" lawyers deserves some discussion on its own.

Government lawyers

Government lawyers often face unique challenges in the practise of the law. Government lawyers often wear three hats: public servant, lawyer, and salaried employee. They work in different operational contexts – ministries, municipal agencies, and often under terms and conditions of employment issued by the employer. However, the common thread for government counsel is that their salaries and benefits are paid from public funds, they are subject to terms and conditions set by the employer, and the "public interest" informs their duties.

Working in the public service may be more demanding. The general expectation is that anyone who works in the public service must always uphold certain values such as even handedness, proportionality and non-discrimination. It is perhaps debatable that the values of a government lawyer are shaped by different considerations. Admittedly, private lawyers have some leg room to advance their interests unhampered by broader concepts of public interests. Inevitably, government lawyers, being paid by the tax payer and representing an elected government have to bear in mind community interests that define and animate public service.

Government lawyers are often called upon to provide advice and representation in a number of areas, often controversial, and with high public policy content. The bottom line however is that the lawyer in public service or employment must not act contrary to public morality, public good, public conscience, public policy, equity and good conscience.

The need to always be fair and reflect public interest is perhaps reflected in the duty of a prosecutor. As is common in many jurisdictions a public prosecutor should not institute or cause to be instituted a criminal charge if he knows or reasonably knows that the charge is not supported by credible evidence.

Furthermore, a public prosecutor should not suppress facts or conceal evidence in order to achieve a conviction. If he knows of any facts or evidence that tends to suggest that the accused is innocent, he must disclose it to the court or to the defence.

The duty owed to the public by the public counsel therefore, is huge and must be faithfully, truthfully and diligently carried out. Other than the constraints referred to above, lawyers in government or its agencies, are still bound to respect their ethical obligations. They too are required to be independent minded and may not be forced to take up a case which they consider would amount to abuse of Court process or otherwise unmeritorious.

Independence from Client and Professional Detachment

Independence of a lawyer means he must avoid self-interest in a matter in which he has been engaged by a client. Factors such as private and personal interests may interfere with the lawyer's objectivity and independence. Quiet often a lawyer's financial interest may conflict with the lawyer's duties towards his or her client. Conflicting self-interest may interfere with the lawyer's professional responsibilities. As a general rule, a conflict of interest, would arise in a situation where a lawyer's ability to represent the client is materially limited by his or her own interests or the interests of third parties.

A Lawyers business interests that may interfere with a Lawyer's Professional judgment

The following may cloud the lawyer's professional judgment:

1. The involvement of the lawyer in a business transaction with the client absent proper disclosure and client consent;

2. Where the lawyer becomes involved in a business, occupation on activity whilst acting for a client and such an interest takes or is likely to take precedence over the client's interest;

3. Unless otherwise authorized by law, knowingly acquiring an ownership, possessory or security interest adverse to the client; and

4. Holding or acquiring a financial interest in the subject matter of a case which the lawyer is conducting, whether or not before a court or administrative body, except, where authorized by law, for contingent fee agreements and liens to secure fees.

Conclusion

Independence is core to an efficient and effective legal profession. It should never be compromised. Although a lawyer must perform his duties independently and without fear he should not at any stage subvert the cause of justice or be unduly overzealous in pursuing the interests of his client.

CHAPTER EIGHT
DRESS CODE FOR LAWYERS

The way in which a lawyer is dressed either gives a good impression of that lawyer or it does not. In court lawyers are expected to be dressed appropriately, invariably, white shirt/blouse, white jabot and dark suit or outfit. It does not reflect very well on a lawyer when the shirt/blouse or jabot are increasingly growing cream or not fitting or about to fall to the ground. It communicates the idea of a lawyer who is casual and not organized.

Appearance in court

Appearing in Court in a multi-coloured outfit is inappropriate. This applies to both men and women. For women, subtle make up is acceptable. In my early days at the bar judges would object to wearing jewellery, but now the courts are a little bit tolerant and not as conservative as in the old days, but even then, it must be done in moderation. No lawyer should be like a Xmas tree in Court! I learnt the hard way, quite early at law school, the importance of dressing conservatively and in dark suit or outfit.

A lesson never to be forgotten

When I was doing my final year at Law School, I was fortunate to be part of the Chief Justice Medal of Advocacy competitions, in which the best performing student won a prize for being a good advocate. The competitions took place at the High Court and a judge presided. I came dressed in a brown suit and I paid the price. Confidently rising to introduce myself, the judge wasted no time in enforcing the standards. He said: "I can't see you". I was confused and didn't know what that meant. In simple terms the judge was saying I was not properly dressed. I was not permitted to address the court and became the first casualty of the competition from the word go because I was not properly dressed. These days as judges we have become quite lenient to lawyers who come to court not properly dressed and in so doing become complicit in the deterioration of standards in the legal profession.

These days, lawyers do not appear to care much about how they dress and appear in Court. The decline is aided by judges who are not calling lawyers to order or sanctioning them by refusing to give them audience on the basis that they are "improperly dressed". A lawyer's appearance must be appropriate, professional and inspire confidence.

Lawyers spend a significant amount of time in office and in court and other public locations (e.g interviews with clients, research at a library, etc.). They must therefore appear professional. Earlier I said it is advisable that lawyers should dress conservatively. What I meant by that is that they should wear dark suits, which includes, black, grey and navy blue. They should also wear appropriate shoes. Leather dress shoes are the legal industry's standard that can be paired with black, grey or navy socks depending on the suit colour. Some colour coordination is ideal but should not be a matter of real concern, unless it is really an eye sore.

Dress code for female lawyers

The dress code for female lawyers is not fundamentally different from that of male lawyers. In the history of law practice, in many jurisdictions, women were predominantly providing legal support and working mainly as secretaries or clerks. However, in the recent past, there has been an increase in female lawyers which has led to some further discussions over what a woman should and should not be wearing. The bottom line is that the dress code should be one that is consistent with the expectations of the profession. For instance, tight fitting clothing, informal stretch pants, mini-skirts are not, in my considered view, acceptable. In my mind females should follow similar guidelines that define male lawyer's dress code.

The general appearance of lawyers is important. Lawyers are expected to be well-groomed when appearing in Court. In regards to hairstyle, neat and conservative hair style is commendable. The bottom line is that the lawyer should look neat and professional. Arriving in a business meeting or court in bright colours is not in keeping with the standards of a profession that is intrinsically conservative.

Accessories, such as watches and jewellery are acceptable if they are not too extravagant. Extravagance may be a question of degree. Wearing too much makeup or revealing tattoos, may not be a good idea. It is important that in enforcing dress code of lawyers the legal profession or judges should not fall into old fashioned gender stereotypes that are prejudicial to women.

Traditionally lawyers always carry briefcases – often black in colour. Briefcases play an important part of a lawyer's job. Having the right briefcase to carry legal documents and files and carefully selected authorities for the day makes the lawyer look professional and organised.

Conclusion

It is important that the legal fraternity should continue to inculcate and deepen those values that define the profession. Dress code is part of those values. Lawyers must at all times maintain the image and professionalism expected of lawyers if they are to earn the respect of their peers and the general public.

A dress code that is not in keeping with the expectation of the profession may bring the profession into disrepute and is therefore undesirable.

CHAPTER NINE

HONESTY, INTEGRITY AND FAIRNESS

The principles of honesty, integrity and fairness underpins the practice of law. Lawyers should act with common courtesy to each other, be fair at all times and seek to catalyse the efficient administration of justice. They are required to be loyal to their clients. One ethical dilemma faced by lawyers is how best to remain loyal to the client, take every advantage in his or her favour, and maintain confidentiality while also fulfilling one's duty of honesty to the court.

Maintaining the above values is necessary if the lawyer is to be trusted by clients, third parties, the courts and the state. This means that the lawyer "must not engage in disgraceful conduct, whether in legal practice or in other business activities or even in private life, of a sort likely to dishonour the profession. One of the most important principles in any effective legal system is that a lawyer is first and foremost an officer of the court or a minister of justice. This principle provides that a lawyer must never knowingly give false or misleading information to the Court, nor should he ever lie to third parties in the course of his or her professional activities.

Lawyers are expected to be honest and fair. They should not litigate in bad faith or knowingly or recklessly mislead the court. Integrity is essential to an efficient and effective legal profession. They must observe common courtesy to their colleagues and to the court. They must be respectful to other court users including witnesses and court staff.

A lawyer may carry on the practice of law so as to be able to earn the respect of his peers and more particularly the courts. This means that in instances when the client asks the lawyer to compromise his or her duties to the court and fair administration of justice in order to put forward a dishonest case, the lawyer's duty to the court prevails. A lawyer should always treat the judge and the court with respect and obey all protocols that promote fairness and impartiality. For instance a lawyer must not make contact with the judge without first informing the lawyer acting for the opposing party or submit exhibits, notes or documents to the judge without communicating them in good time to the lawyer on the other side unless such steps are permitted under the relevant rules of procedure.

The duty of honesty and integrity precludes the lawyer from engaging in conduct that involves the conscious dissemination of untruths or making denigrating statements concerning other lawyers, the court or the person of the judge.

The duty of honesty also requires that lawyers should refrain from furnishing factual information which they know or should have known to be incorrect. Lawyers must avoid expressing themselves in offensive terms and must take into account the interests of the other party and any third party. Lawyers must avoid contacting a party on a matter in respect of which they know this party has a lawyer or seek to prevail upon the client of another lawyer to settle a matter or otherwise concede anything.

As a general rule there is no expectation that the lawyer should vouch to the truthfulness of the witness's testimony in court. However, he should not be a party, to a situation in which, the witness, to his knowledge is misleading the court by presenting false testimony.

Lawyers are ethically bound to be fair to opposing party. This means that the lawyer must not, for example, unlawfully obstruct another party's access to evidence, destroy or conceal any documents with evidentiary value, make frivolous requests, or assert personal knowledge of facts.

The duty to act with honesty and integrity includes several requirements. Under these requirements, a lawyer must not knowingly or recklessly mislead or attempt to mislead anyone or encourage witnesses to testify in a misleading or untruthful manner, or rehearse, practice with or coach witnesses.

The duty to be fair requires, among other things, that lawyers litigate honestly and in good truth. It requires the lawyer to be fair to his opponent, to cooperate and allow discoveries that are permissible under the rules of court and not to destroy or unseal any documents that can assist the court to come to a fair determination of the matter before it.

In the case *Rondel v Worlsey* (1969) 1 AC 191, 227 Lord Reid explained the lawyer's duty to the client and to the court in the following terms:

> *Every counsel has a duty to his client fearlessly, to raise every issue, advance every argument and ask every question, however distasteful, which he thinks will help his client's case. But, as an officer of the court concerned in the administration of justice, he has an overriding duty to the court, to the standards of his profession, and to the public, which may and often does lead to a conflict with his client's wishes or with what the client thinks are his personal interests. Counsel must not mislead the court, he must not lend himself to casting aspersions on the other party or witnesses for which there is no sufficient basis in the information in his possession, he must not withhold authorities or documents which may tell against his clients but which the law or the standards of his profession require him to produce.*

Lawyers must consciously abstain from offensive and discreditable conduct towards all players in the justice system, such as intimidation, harassment and dishonesty. It is unethical not to tell the truth because you want a particular result for a client.

A lawyer's relationship to the opposing party and colleagues must be one of honesty, integrity and fairness. For instance, a lawyer must not see an enemy in the opposing party but just an opponent who might believe to be right just like the client the lawyer is representing.

A lawyer must not take advantage of an unrepresented litigant. The lawyer's duties of honesty, integrity and fairness prohibit taking advantage, in anyway whatsoever, of unrepresented litigant, such as for instance persuading him to withdraw a matter and otherwise making concessions which would be inappropriate and against his interest using the opponent's lack of knowledge in order to obtain unfair success for the client.

The core duties of honesty, integrity and fairness require maintaining honesty and trust in relations with the client, respect for the fair administration of justice and treating colleagues, including the opposing lawyers, with respect and courtesy. A lawyer who is dishonest, litigates in bath faith, is discourteous to colleagues and the court may suffer reputational damage and find the practice of law cumbersome or otherwise unpleasant.

Conclusion

The duty of honesty and integrity requires that a lawyer must keep the client updated about the progress of the case and honestly explain to the client the causes of the delay. This requires that the lawyer must own up to any delays occasioned by him and not to dishonestly attribute the delay to the court staff or a judge when it is not true that they are the cause of the delay. And lawyers should not abuse the lack of knowledge of unrepresented litigants in order to obtain unfair advantage for their client.

CHAPTER TEN

A LAWYER'S DUTY TO THE CLIENT

Loyalty and the ability to act in the best interests of the client are essential elements of the lawyer-client relationship. Once a lawyer takes on the case, the principle of loyalty prohibits withdrawing from the case when the case seems complicated or destined to fail. Loyalty requires lawyers to fulfil their duties with commitment and dedication.

A lawyer must always act in the best interests of the client and must put those interests before his/her own interests or those of fellow members of the legal profession. However, it must be noted that a lawyer's duty of loyalty to the client is subject to due observance of the law and rules of professional conduct. To be loyal means that the lawyer must be independent, avoid conflict of interest and keep a client's confidence. Loyalty also requires a lawyer to act promptly on a client's interests.

Loyalty is the essence of a lawyer's duty to a client. It means acting in the best interest of the client. It is one of the values that constitute the fundamental principles of the profession.

The duty of loyalty includes being competent and carrying out the assignment or mandate of a client with extreme care and diligence. The duty of loyalty obliges the lawyer to avoid conflict of interest situations and to respect the principle of confidentiality discussed earlier.

In the practice of law there are a number of possible conflicts which I discuss hereunder.

Acting for both Parties

As a general rule acting for two (2) clients with opposing interests should not be done. This is so because the lawyer owes a fiduciary duty to respect the confidences of clients and at the same time to do his or her best for the client. If a lawyer acts in a manner that disadvantages another client he/she may open himself/herself to being sued for malpractice, or removed from the roll of practising lawyers.

Some lawyers often seek to conceal a conflict of interest by suggesting that clients with diametrically opposed interests are represented by different lawyers in the same firm and that in consequence there is no conflict. In my view it does not make a difference if two members of the same law firm represent two clients with diametrically opposed interests against each other.

A law firm cannot hide under the corporate veil to avoid conflict of interest and to proceed to have its partners or associates to act for separate clients whose interests are diametrically opposed. If it purports to continue to act for both clients by imposing a qualification on the duties of partnership it thereby denies the respective clients the services the clients have sought from the firm, namely the delivery of such uncompromised professional skill and advice as the partnership is able to provide. In such a situation the picture painted to the public is that the interests of the firm are in conflict with, and may be preferred to, the interest of one or both clients. It is an undesirable situation. It must be avoided at all costs.

The lawyer, the client and vested interests

It is good practice for lawyers to desist from having business dealings with a client. This kind of situation is pregnant with possible conflict of interests. The lawyer cannot in good conscience be the lawyer and a shareholder of a company that is litigating in court.

Where there is any conflict between the interests of the client and that of the lawyer, the lawyer has a duty to act in perfect good faith and to make full disclosure of his interest. It must be a conscientious disclosure of all material circumstances, and everything known to him relating to the proposed transaction which might influence the conduct of the client or anybody from whom he might seek advice.

Opposing a former Client

The question of opposing a former client depends in large part on information the lawyer has that may be used against the former client. At the end of the day it is a question of assessing risk.

The common law position concerning the test for disqualification on the basis of a conflict of interest involving a former client is whether there is a reasonable probability of real mischief. Where there is a risk of possible conflict, but the lawyer seems ready to ignore same the court should intervene in the interests of justice. The risk should be a real one, and not merely fanciful or farfetched. I prefer saying the risk although not substantial should at the very least be significant. But it need not be substantial. As a general rule a lawyer should not, without the consent of his former client, accept instructions unless, viewed objectively, his doing so will not increase the risk that information which is confidential to the former client may come into the possession of a party with an adverse interest.

The courts should be careful to ensure that former clients are not otherwise exposed to potential and avoidable risks to which they had not consented.

Conclusion

The principle of loyalty lies at the heart of the lawyer's duties to clients. Loyalty creates the trust the enables effective representation. All other aspects of the lawyer-client relationship, such as avoiding the conflict of interests, maintaining confidentiality and independence derive from and reinforce the lawyer's primary duty of loyalty. A breach of the principles of loyalty would most certainly render the lawyer-client relationship untenable.

CHAPTER ELEVEN
CONFIDENTIALITY

The duty of observing confidentiality that a lawyer owes to a client is paramount. Clients entrust lawyers with sensitive information and in so doing they do not expect a lawyer to share the information with third parties.

The client must feel free to confide in his lawyer and that such information entrusted to his lawyer is safe. The duty of confidence also gives rise to an ethical obligation and thus a breach of client confidentially would be grounds for disciplinary action. There are exceptions, such as where the client consents, or where the lawyer is compelled by law to disclose, or where the wider public interest requires disclosure.

The principle of confidentiality is one of the core duties of a lawyer to his client. The principle of confidentiality encourages the frank and full communication between lawyers and their clients. It ensures that trust characterizes the lawyer-client relationship and assists the lawyer in providing effective legal representation to a client.

The essence of confidentiality

Essentially confidentiality refers to the duty of the lawyer to keep clients' matters confidential and to respect professional secrecy. The principle of confidentiality has a dual nature: on the one hand it is the lawyer's duty to observe confidentiality; on the other hand it is a fundamental human right of the client. The duty of confidentiality prohibits a client's communication from being divulged to unauthorized parties.

The principle of confidentiality is an indispensable feature of the rule of law. It is equally essential to public trust and confidence in the administration of justice and the independence of the legal profession. It has two main features. First, it is the contractual, ethical and frequently statutory duty on the part of the lawyer to keep client secrets confidential.

The purpose of confidentiality

The principle of confidentiality is meant to protect the client and the integrity of the legal profession. A lawyer cannot invoke the principle of confidentiality to shield himself from criminal responsibility. He can also not invoke the principle in order to aid and abet the commission of a crime by his client. A lawyer cannot act as an accomplice to crime and turn around to invoke the principle of confidentiality. In some jurisdictions, legislation has been passed imposing a duty on lawyers to assist in the prevention of crime, such as terrorism and money laundering.

Jurisdictions, such as in France, a breach of a lawyer's duty of confidentiality to a client is a criminal offence. The duty of confidentiality is generally absolute and unlimited in time, save where the law provides for some exceptions or prescribes a time period. It subsists long after the lawyer has ceased acting for a client.

Scope

The duty of confidentiality covers communications protected by the lawyer-client privilege, plus any other information relating to the representation. Unlike the lawyer-client privilege, which protects only confidential communications between the lawyer and client, the ethical duty of confidentiality protects information regardless of the source.

Generally, the lawyer-client privilege does not apply in situations when:

- it is used to engage or assist in a crime or fraud, commonly referred to as the "crime-fraud exception;
- the confidential communications are relevant to the dispute arising out of the breach of the lawyer-client relationship;

The exceptions to the ethical duty of confidentiality are where:

- the client gives an informed consent to reveal the confidential information;
- the lawyer needs to protect himself or herself against a claim for malpractice, disciplinary violation, or the like;
- the disclosure is required by the law or court;

☐ the lawyer reasonably believes that the disclosure is necessary to prevent certain death or substantial bodily harm;

Conclusion

Confidentiality of the lawyer-client communication is an essential aspect of the lawyer's work. The client must feel confident that his or her highly sensitive information will not fall into the wrong hands. Lawyers should be aware of the boundaries and exception(s) to their duties regarding confidentiality, as well as the lawyer-client privilege in order to most effectively advise their clients.

CHAPTER TWELVE

CONFLICT OF INTEREST

It is well settled that a lawyer has a fiduciary duty to his or her client. That duty carries with it two responsibilities. The first is the obligation to avoid any conflict between his duty to his client and his own interests – he must not make a profit or secure a benefit, at the expense of his client.

One Master at a time

A lawyer can only serve one master at a time. To serve two masters at a time is a powder keg and must be avoided at all times. Conflicts of interest are not all that easy to resolve because some interests will require that the lawyer not act for the person while other conflicts may still allow for the lawyer to act for both parties. At the end of the day, it is safe that where it appears that there is a conflict the lawyer should act in a manner as to avoid the conflict. The second responsibility?

In the practice of law conflict of interest is all too common. Lawyers frequently find themselves in situations where the client's interests conflict with the lawyer's responsibilities to another client, to a former client, to third parties, or even against the lawyer's own personal interests. As a general rule, a conflict of interest exists when a lawyer's ability to represent the client is seriously compromised by his or her own interests or the interests of third parties. There are many types of conflicts of interest. Common examples include conflicts between the lawyer and client, among the lawyer's concurrent clients, among the current and former clients, and conflicts due to the lawyer's duties to the third parties.

Generally, it is prudent for a lawyer to avoid:

- ☐ Representing two or more clients in the same matter if there is a conflict, or a significant risk of conflict, between the interests of those clients;

- ☐ Representing both or all of the clients concerned when a conflict of interests arises between those clients and also whenever there is a risk of a breach of confidence;

- ☐ Representing a new client if there is a risk of breach of confidence entrusted to the lawyer by a former client or if the knowledge which the lawyer possesses of the affairs of the former client would give an undue advantage to the new client.

It must be said, however, that it is possible for a lawyer or a firm of lawyers to represent two or more clients in the same matter if there is no conflict or risk of any conflict.

A lawyer should not assume a position in which a client's interests conflict with those of the lawyer, another lawyer in the same firm, or another client, unless it is permitted by law or the client has given his consent.

It should be stated for avoidance of doubt that if a conflict only becomes apparent after a lawyer has assumed agency and has started to work on a matter, he must as soon as he realises a conflict withdraw from such a matter.

Waiver

It is generally accepted that no conflict exists in a situation where a lawyer informs the client of the conflict, but the client nevertheless instructs him to proceed. In these circumstances it may be prudent to record such disclosure and agreement in some detail and in writing.

In other words a conflict of interest may be waived in situations where the client consents following comprehensive information, to be represented by the lawyer and where this is not against the interests of the proper administration of justice.

Examples of conflict of interest

There are a number of situations in which conflict of interest often arises. These are where:

- a lawyer enters into a business or financial transaction with the client;

- a lawyer's personal interests may affect the representation of the client, such as a relationship with the opposing party or when the related persons (spouses, siblings, etc) represent the adverse parties;

- a lawyer drafts an instrument, for example, a will, in which a client who is not related to the lawyer gives a gift to the lawyer or his or her close relative.

If a client consent to what may otherwise be a conflict of interest the lawyer must ensure that the consent of the client is informed. This could only happen in a situation where the lawyer gives the client comprehensive and relevant information to facilitate informed consent.

Conclusion

There is no uniform definition of "conflict of interest". It is therefore possible that jurisdictions may differ as to what constitutes conflict of interest. However, and as a general rule conflicts of interest exist when a lawyer's representation of a client is compromised by his or her obligations to a third party, or by the lawyer's self-interest.

CHAPTER THIRTEEN
DILIGENCE

The obligation of a lawyer to be diligent in carrying out the instructions of a client covers a multitude of circumstances. A lawyer is an expert in the law. The clients seek his counsel or opinion on the law because of his/her expertise. In discharging his duties he must exercise requisite competence and care. Breach of competence and care can give rise to an action against the lawyer for damages as well as lead to disciplinary action. The duty of care and competence requires a lawyer to maintain professional standards at all times.

Minimum standards

The minimum standards that a lawyer should subscribe to include basic legal knowledge, and also to keep abreast of the law in his field of practice. It is therefore absolutely important that a lawyer must be knowledgeable about both procedural and substantive law. Clients desire and expect competent legal representation. Competent representation requires not only legal knowledge and skill, but thorough preparation reasonably necessary for a Court to decide a matter favourably. Determining whether a lawyer is competent or not is not easy. However relevant considerations include basic knowledge of both substantive and procedural law; preparation and the ability to efficiently and effectively represent the client in court.

Fair Trial

The duty of diligence is important in ensuring that the client receives a fair trial and effective assistance. It is wrong for a lawyer to handle a matter with respect to which he has no competence and is unlikely to properly advise a client. Once a lawyer has accepted instructions he must do his best to advance the client's case. He cannot just withdraw from a matter without informing the client and for a good reason and complying with the rules governing withdrawals of lawyers.

A lawyer owes a duty of care to his client, breach of which may result in the lawyer being sued. This duty requires a lawyer to properly assess the facts of the case and the law, paying due regard to binding precedent in relation to the subject of matter of the litigation and to provide intelligent, meaningful and sound legal advice which is supported by authorities.

Nature of Instructions

The lawyer is required to establish the nature of his instructions. If he has reason to suspect that the instructions are intended to assist in the commission of an offence, the lawyer must immediately seek to dissuade his client. If this fails, the lawyer must withdraw from the case.

The duty of diligence requires a lawyer to act with promptness; to be efficient and do his best despite opposition or personal inconvenience. Diligence requires that lawyers provide their clients with competent standards of work and be fair and independent in advancing the interests of the client. He must not allow a matter to prescribe following instructions or take a matter that has prescribed.

Unnecessary postponements

A lawyer should be weary of unnecessary postponements that simply increase costs of a client and enrich the lawyer. In appropriate cases judges may condemn lawyers who are unduly delaying matters by ordering them to pay costs. In a number of cases costs are awarded against the client although the cause of the delay is the lawyer.

In most jurisdictions the law makes provision for the discipline of lawyers for any misconduct. The law typically makes provision for an allegation or complaint of professional misconduct. Law societies are the professional bodies that are often established to ensure that lawyers perform their duties professionally. Being professional requires that lawyers be properly qualified and subscribe to set standards that govern the practice of law.

Conclusion

Diligence is important to the work of a lawyer. No client would instruct a lawyer who he knows to be incompetent.

The nature of legal practice where failure to comply with time lines may be fatal to a client's cause means that lawyers must at all times be efficient and manage their diaries in a manner that enables them to comply with court orders. I know of many lawyers who are always late in court. These lawyers other than placing the interests of their clients at risk are also risking their reputations and bringing disrepute to their profession.

CHAPTER FOURTEEN
PROFESSIONAL NEGLIGENCE

The issue of whether a lawyer is liable to a client for damages occasioned by professional negligence has a chequered path.

Liability for negligence

For decades following English law, a lawyer was said not to be responsible for any mistake, indiscretion or error of judgment of any sort. However, in 1964, with the introduction of liability for negligent statements by the House of Lords in *Hedley Byrne & Co. Ltd v Heller and Partners* (the 1964 AC 465) the continued existence of such an immunity became questionable. Three years later in 1967 in the case of *Rondel v Worsely* (1969 AC 191), the House of Lords put such doubts to rest by holding unanimously that a lawyer was entitled to some immunity from actions in respect of professional negligence, specifically those arising from the conduct of proceedings in court.

In effect, the Court held that to hold a lawyer liable for professional negligence runs counter to public interest. They seemed to rely on three broad grounds of public interest:

a) A lawyer owes a duty to the court which must be carried out fearlessly and independently. The duty is superior to any duty he may owe his client.

b) An action for negligence against a lawyer would involve a re-trial of the original case which would result in expensive litigation.

c) A lawyer is under an obligation to accept any client, who seeks his services, even those he may consider undeserving.

Almost a decade later, in 1978, in *Saif Alt v Sydney Mitchell & Co.* (1978 3 ALL ER page), the House of Lords were asked to rule on the extent of a lawyer's immunity (and not as to whether a lawyer has immunity at all against a professional negligence suit). The Court, held that although the lawyer enjoys immunity, such immunity is not absolute.

The general protection of a lawyer was said to be only available if the particular work was connected to the way a matter was to be conducted when it comes to be heard in Court. In other words liability was confined to the conduct of litigation.

In most jurisdictions, in the contemporary era, at least in the common law countries, it is now acknowledged that lawyers are liable for professional negligence to their clients. I have presided over numerous cases where I have held lawyers liable for shoddy prosecution of a client's case leading to unwarranted dismissal. Most of these cases relate to a lawyer being instructed to initiate litigation before a matter prescribed, but a lawyer then unjustifiably sitting on the matter until it prescribes.

It cannot be correct and it would offend against justice that a dissatisfied client whose lawyer has not carried out his mandate diligently, resulting in unwarranted loss should go without a remedy. Any unnecessary expense occasioned to a client by a lawyer, like a lawyer failing to appear at a trial and the matter being dismissed as a result, should ordinarily be claimable from a lawyer by the client.

In a few cases that came before me in the last 18 years (I remember about five) concerning a lawyer's negligence, no lawyer has sought to invoke immunity as a defence. If anything at all, they have pleaded contributory negligence, such as where a lawyer says he was instructed a few days before a matter prescribed. It seems to me that it would be offensive to fairness and accountability to shield a lawyer who is guilty of malpractice. The problem of lawyer's malpractice is of special concern to the public at large for it puts into doubt the very efficiency and quality of the legal process; factors which are of critical importance in fostering and retaining the requisite degree of respect for the law and the legal system.

Nevertheless, whatever rigorous standards or elaborate safeguards are maintained by the legal system, it would be naive and unrealistic to claim that there are no faultless lawyers and that all lawyers are masters of their craft. The fact that most clients place themselves entirely within the control and discretion of their lawyers is to be weighted heavily in deciding on the course and measures to be taken when there is an occasional and inevitable breakdown in that relationship.

In my mind the continued integrity and well-being of the legal system demands that such instances be dealt with not by unduly protecting lawyers. In fact one can credibly say public policy requires that the lawyers must be made to pay for professional negligence in as much as other professions like doctors do. A lawyer's malpractice discredits the law and the administration of justice. It harms the public. Where a lawyer's negligence deprives a client of a benefit such as property or insurance policy, damage is done to the client and public confidence in the ability of the law to safeguard individual and public interest.

Immunity

The reason why a lawyer should not be immune is that he holds himself out as professional possessing requisite skills, in particular that he has the ability to conduct litigation with skill and knowledge. Accordingly, he should be treated in the same manner as other professionals and owe a similar duty of care to his clients. Secondly, there is no basis to suggest that the disastrous consequences anticipated by certain judges and commentators, namely, a proliferation of disputes between accusing clients and accused lawyers would flow from discarding immunity and ought to be rejected. The fear of a deluge of negligence actions is a groundless one.

It seems to me that holding lawyers to account will go a long way in providing an incentive for them to improve the quality of work or services they render. The overwhelming jurisprudence in the commonwealth, as far as I am able to discern, seems to suggest that a lawyer must exercise reasonable care, skill and knowledge in the conduct of litigation and must be diligent in prosecuting a client's case. Gone are the days he could plead immunity and be allowed to go scot free.

In my mind, it cannot be argued that without such immunity, the lawyer is vulnerable, exposed and without any defence against the disgruntled client. The lawyer would not be liable for the smallest mistake or error of judgment. His conduct would not be adjudged against some absolute standard, but would be measured against that of a prudent and ordinarily competent lawyer, following the customary practise adopted by the profession. (*Aaroe v Seymour* [1956] O.R 736 [C.A])

The standard

In professional negligent cases the lawyer's conduct is measured against that of a prudent and ordinarily competent lawyer. This standard was articulated correctly by Lord Diplock in the case of *Saif Ali*, cited earlier when he said:

> *"Those who hold themselves out as qualified to practise..., although they are not liable for damage caused by what in the event turns out to have been an error of judgment on some matter upon which*

the opinions of reasonably informed and competent members of the profession might have differed, are nevertheless liable for damage caused by their advice, acts or omissions in the course of their professional work which no member of the profession who was reasonably well-informed and competent would have given or done or omitted to do."

Conclusion

The last thing any client expects is to engage a lawyer who is not diligent and engages in conduct that causes harm to him. In such a situation the law must step in. Unfortunately, it is all too common for lawyers to make costly mistakes, miss deadlines and give wrong advice to clients. It is therefore appropriate that clients who suffer damages because of a lawyer's breach of duty of care and attention, incompetence and negligence should have a remedy. This is the same as an engineer who provides a client with flawed designs that ultimately causes harm. Such an engineer should not escape liability.

CHAPTER FIFTEEN

PREPARING AND PRESENTING EVIDENCE IN COURT

Evidence at a trial may be given orally or by affidavit. Leading evidence in court may involve witness preparation. Witnesses must understand that a trial is about finding the truth. As everyone familiar with a trial would testify, fact finding in a trial is an extremely complex affair.

Nothing but the truth

It is important that witnesses must always tell the court the truth. Lies can hardly survive focused and sustained cross examination. They crumble even under mild but sustained cross examination. It is therefore true that whilst a lawyer can attempt to dress up bad facts, so as to look not as bad, he cannot resuscitate a case caught up in a web of lies. Such a case is likely to crumble spectacularly. There is no doubt that telling lies would affect the case of a party who calls the lying witness adversely.

All those experienced in conducting trails would confirm that sometime truth is relative. And as it is often said, "the pure and simple truth is rarely pure and never simple". The law does not permit lawyers to prepare witness for trial so as to tell falsehoods to the Court. Witnesses' preparation must therefore be ethical. Inevitably witnesses preparation come with ethical dilemmas – namely the potential conflict between the duty to the court to act with honesty and candour, and the duty to represent a client competently and diligently.

No coaching is allowed

Lawyers are not allowed to suggest answers to witnesses. It is normal for a lawyer to admonish a witness to tell the truth or challenge his testimony by pointing out inconsistencies in his evidence. But under no circumstances should a lawyer encourage a witness to give evidence which the witness believes to be untrue.

Probing a witness or pointing out the inconsistencies in his evidence should not be aimed at convincing the witness to change that which he knows to be true. To do so would be improper. Admittedly challenging inconsistencies in the witnesses testimony may convey the impression to the witness that they are somehow wrong as to their recollection or that it is in their best interests to adapt their testimony. Lawyers need to guard against this impression. It is therefore incumbent upon a lawyer to be very clear about one thing: the importance of telling the truth. It is usually a good idea to exhaust the witness's recollection of events first, before seeking to test them. In this way the lawyer does not inadvertently alter the witnesses' testimony. Exhausting the witness's recollection may require a lawyer to ask open-ended questions that do not suggest a particular answer and begin with broad general questions and then narrow down to particular issues.

During my days in practice, I was very particular in ensuring that during the course of taking instructions and probing the witness I did not come across as encouraging the witness to lie. Where there were many witnesses I would in fact caution them against discussing their evidence and caucusing on what to say. In circumstances where I would not be satisfied, that a particular witness would add value to the trial, I would not call that witness. This is a tactical decision that a lawyer is permitted to take.

Once, whilst presiding in a trial in Kokopo, Papua New Guinea, it became clear to me that the lawyer may have coached witnesses when they all deposed to identical facts in an affidavit estimating that a particular driver, in a motor vehicle accident case, was driving at a speeding of 60km/h. Not all these witnesses were in the same car or same place. Some were in the car and others just onlookers who happened to be at the location where the accident took place. Yet their estimation of the speed was identical. It was obvious to me that they were coached and the evidence was not credible at all. I rejected it accordingly.

Listening

Listening to what is being asked by a lawyer or judge in the course of a trial is important. Strangely many witnesses tend to give the impression that they were not listening attentively. The fact of the matter is that if witnesses do not pay attention or think they are being asked about one thing when another is intended, matters can become confused and a case muddled up and even lost. It follows from the above that it is good practice to advise witnesses to listen to the question carefully before answering. Next a witness should be told to make sure they understand the question. If they do not understand the question, then they should say so and ask the questioner to explain, repeat or rephrase the question. It may be dangerous to proceed to answer the question that is vague and even irrelevant. Witnesses should also be careful about certain types of questions that a lawyer may ask deliberately, such as questions that purport to summarise earlier testimony, which include imprecise language. The witness does not need to be argumentative but should make sure that their understanding of a word or concept is the same as that of the lawyer asking the questions.

Decades of experience at the service of the law has also taught me that saying too much is often counter-productive at a trial. Witnesses must learn to say only what is necessary and relevant to the issues being tried.

Golden rules

In a trial witnesses must heed the following golden rules:

- Answer clearly and succinctly;
- If you don't know the answer, say "I don't know," or if you don't remember the answer, say "I don't remember" but don't confuse the two as not

remembering implies that you did know the answer at some point in the past;

- Don't speculate, guess or assume. Listen carefully and understand the question;
- Do not volunteer information, answer only the question asked; and
- Correct mistakes and if you realize you have been inaccurate or incomplete, say so.

It is also a notorious fact that quite often, in an attempt to squeeze or box a witness to give a convenient answer lawyers would plead with the witness to simply say: "Yes" or "No". Witnesses need not blindly comply. A witness should feel free to convey the difficulty to the Court by saying it is a not a yes or no, black or white answer and seek the Court's permission to explain what he means. However there are often questions that are clearly amenable to a "yes or no" answer.

Nature of evidence

Evidence in Court may be either oral or documentary. Documentary evidence is often more reliable than oral evidence. Most judges I know will give far greater weight to a document created contemporaneously with an event, the subject of litigation, than witnesses' recollections. Human experience teaches that oral testimony of evidence given many years ago may not be reliable as memories tend to fade with time. In commercial transactions it is much safer to rely on documentary evidence. Documentary evidence is to be preferred over that of a witness with an interest in the case. Often, because of vested interests, witnesses may put a slant upon events some years after they occurred.

Practice makes perfect

It is often said practice makes perfect. This is true of any trial. In some jurisdictions such as in the US preparation for trial may require witnesses to participate in mock cross examination rehearsals. This is not done in Botswana. The attitude in Botswana and other countries that do not do such mock rehearsals is that the said rehearsals may amount to coaching witnesses to answer questions in a certain way. As earlier said preparation of witnesses that involves general advise to be calm and honest is acceptable. It is also acceptable, in my view for a lawyer to advise a witness to use simple language.

The need for confidentiality should be explained to all witnesses. Lawyers, in the event they are called as witnesses against their former clients, may not disclose the content of lawyer-client consultations. Such confidentiality is absolute. As part of preparing witnesses for a trial a lawyer is at liberty to familiarise himself with the court layout and general environment. Most people hardly attend court. They have absolutely no experience of a number of things, such as where to sit and where to go if called upon to come and lead evidence. Some may feel very intimidated and even oppressed by the court atmosphere. It is therefore a good idea to calm nerves and inform witnesses about these practical matters. It is also a good idea to tell witnesses about basic court procedure. All these would make the witness feel comfortable in court.

It is also advisable to go through the general procedure that will take place in the court, such as being called to testify, being sworn and the sequence of examination, cross-examination and re-examination. If a witness knows what to expect, the better.

Evaluation of witnesses is allowed

There is no prohibition against evaluating witnesses' readiness to testify by asking them whether they understood the procedure and reminding them to be honest in the answers they give. It is also not wrong to say to the witnesses that they need not be fearful or intimidated by the opposing lawyer because if anyone harasses them the court would protect them and that they must always remain calm. This is particularly important because a scared witness is likely to underperform. Most witnesses will be nervous to some degree about testifying. For example, it may be the fear of speaking in court, forgetting some details, not knowing an answer to a question or concern as to how they will hold up under cross-examination.

How to address anxiety would depend on the source of the anxiety but there are a couple of general responses to almost all nervous witnesses. Reassure a witness through explaining that most witnesses share the same concerns but it does not make them unsuitable to testify. In fact a little nervousness is a positive thing because it will mean the witness is on their toes. Explain that the witness preparation process they have been through (or will go through) equips them to deal with testifying. As lay witnesses they are not expected to be experts in courtroom testifying.

It is also not wrong, in my view, to caution the witness not to be over-confident, and to counsel him to concentrate on the questions that are being agued and answer them correctly, regardless of the tone or approach taken by the opposing lawyer. Remind the witnesses that their job is to truthfully answer the questions put to them.

Affidavits

An affidavit is written evidence that is given under oath or affirmation before a Commissioner of Oaths. Affidavits vary in content. They can be detailed substantiation of the evidence or can be merely procedural as with an affidavit verifying pleadings or a list of documents and affidavits of service. Below I give a general outline of basic features of an affidavit that lawyers must always bear in mind.

Legal requirements for Affidavits

All affidavits must be sworn or affirmed. An affidavit is sworn when it is taken on oath. An affirmation substitutes the words "solemnly, sincerely and truly declare and affirm" for the word "swear" or for any other word or words to the like effect and omitting the words "so help me God". An affidavit may be sworn or affirmed before a Commissioner of Oaths.

Typically, where a deponent chooses to take an oath, whether by using a holy book/religious text, or without it, a diligent Commissioner of Oaths would or may ask: *"Do you swear that the contents of this your affidavit are true and correct to the best of your knowledge and belief?"*

The deponent should swear to the truth of the document by saying: *"I swear that all that I have stated in this affidavit is true, so help me God, or the name of the God recognised by the deponent's religion".*

If the deponent chooses to make an affirmation, the Commissioner of Oaths may ask: *"Do you solemnly and sincerely declare and affirm that the contents of this your affidavit are true and correct to the best of your knowledge and belief?"*

The deponent should then swear to the truth of the contents of the document by saying: *"I do".*

Generally a deponent should be a person who can attest to the truth from their personal knowledge. Put another way, they are not reporting matters told to them by another person, as that would be hearsay. As a general rule hearsay evidence is not admissible unless if permitted by the rules. This may be so in urgent applications or some other circumstances as may be prescribed by law.

Persons who may make Affidavits

1. If more than one person is qualified to make an affidavit on behalf of a party, it is sufficient for such an affidavit to be made by a representative, and the others may verify the facts as they relate to them.

2. Subject to any order of the court, the person by whom an affidavit is made must be a person having knowledge of the facts deposed to in the affidavit.

3. If an affidavit is made by a person other than the party required to file or verify the affidavit, the affidavit must set out the facts that qualify the person to make the affidavit.

Heading to Affidavit

The heading of an affidavit must include the name of the deponent and the date on which the affidavit is made.

Format of Affidavit dealing with more than one matter

If the body of an affidavit alleges or otherwise deals with more than one matter;

a) It must be divided into paragraphs;

b) Each factual allegation must, so far as convenient, be put in a separate paragraph, and

c) The paragraphs must be numbered consecutively.

Alterations

As a general rule, if there is any interlineations, erasure or other alteration in the jurat or body of an affidavit, the affidavit may not be used, except by leave of the court, unless the person before whom the affidavit is sworn initials the alteration.

Annexure

A document to be used in conjunction with an affidavit may be made an annexure to the affidavit. An annexure to an affidavit must be identified as such by a Commissioner of Oaths.

False Swearing

A person before whom an affidavit is made must not permit the swearing of an affidavit that he or she knows is false. He should also not permit an affidavit to be sworn if the person has reason to believe that the deponent does not understand the contents of the affidavit or the nature of an oath or affirmation. It is quite common to read affidavits that contain obvious mistakes that would have been detected had the deponent taken the trouble to read the affidavit before swearing it. Most of the time the mistakes are typographical.

I am often surprised that some lawyers would seek to alter any affidavit to correct what they consider insignificant. That is wrong because it amounts to altering the evidence of a witness.

A lawyer who is responsible for the taking of an affidavit should make sure that the deponent has read and understands its contents. The duty of a person who administers an oath in relation to an affidavit is to satisfy himself or herself that the witness understands that to which the witness is going to swear. Affidavit evidence is as important as oral testimony given in the witness box. It follows that affidavit evidence may only be entitled to the same weight as oral evidence if those who swear affidavits realise that the obligation of the oath is as serious when making an affidavit as it is when making statements in the witness box.

It is not acceptable for lawyers to be involved in the preparation of false affidavits. Even if, at the time when an affidavit is made, a lawyer has no good reasons to suppose that the affidavit is untrue, once he becomes aware that any of the contents of the affidavit may be untrue he must not seek to obtain an order adverse to another on what he knows or has reason to believe is untruthful.

It should be noted that the conscious withholding of information from an affidavit that creates a misleading impression is equally reprehensible.

CHAPTER SIXTEEN
THE ART OF CROSS-EXAMINATION

Cross-examination is one of the most important parts of a trial. Its purpose is not to attack the adversary and make all sorts of abusive imputations to a witness. Its purpose, admittedly, includes discrediting the evidence or version of the opponent, but equally important, to put one's version of the story across. Cross-examination can make or destroy a case. It is the keystone of a successful trial. Cross-examination is in the main a function of experience, and not just reading law books, although the latter may help.

Critical tool for unearthing the truth

Cross examination is critical in the search of the truth in an adversarial system. It allows a party to probe and discredit the evidence given by an adverse witness. Put to good use it can be very helpful. There are perhaps two main purposes of cross-examination: to expose the weaknesses of an adverse witness and to put across your own witness's version of events.

Tireless preparation is key

In my experience the foundation of effective cross-examination is tireless preparation. Effective cross-examination requires knowledge of material facts and the relevant law. A lawyer who intends to embark on an effective and productive cross-examination must carefully take instructions and decipher material facts. More often than not he takes what he is told by client as truthful unless there is some inconsistency in the narration of the facts that gives him the impression that he was not told the whole truth. Where that is so, he must endeavour to set the true facts in order to avoid possible embarrassment during trial.

Whilst a lawyer generally accepts the word of his client as to matters in controversy if his story is reasonable and cohesive, in preparation of his case it is sometimes well to test the client's story, as well as the accounts of his chief witnesses, by subjecting them to the same type of cross-examination they may expect from opposing lawyer. This serves the twin purpose of preparing the witness for possible pitfalls during trial and demonstrating to him the importance of remaining calm under a barrage of hostile questioning.

Cross –examination is not compulsory

Many lawyers seem to think that cross-examination is compulsory and often embark on unnecessary cross-examination. A lawyer is not forced to cross-examine and, indeed, he should not do so unless the witness has damaged his case. A witness who knows what he is talking about and who testifies to the truth is not vulnerable to cross-examination. Sometime to embark on cross-examination routinely may be costly as the witness may give adverse information that he would otherwise not have divulged. It is prudent therefore to let a witness go without being cross-examined, if to do otherwise would not help your case.

Another important rule that is often ignored by many lawyers is that a lawyer should not ask a question unless he is quite sure what the answer will be.

As a rule of thumb witnesses who are unlikely to be shaken in their testimony or contradict themselves should not be cross-examined as that may only serve to reinforce their testimony through questioning. Accordingly before deciding to cross examine a witness, evaluate whether it is worth doing so at all.

In deciding to cross-examine a witness, you must be clear in your mind what the cross examination is intended to achieve. It is of critical importance to have a cross-examination plan and to know where you are going, because, as it is often said, "if you don't know where you are going, wherever you arrive would be the destination", which most likely be the place you never intended to go, with possible adverse consequences.

A cross-examination plan is essential

I cannot emphasise more than I have already done that a lawyer must have a cross-examination plan. At the very minimum a lawyer must have a written outline of the points he wants to make. A lawyer who fumbles as he tries to cross examine may end up destroying his client's case. The more a lawyer can tie cross-examination to certain material facts and not just any point the better.

It is a good practice not to engage in disjointed and confusing cross-examination, which often betrays lack of appreciation of the real issues in controversy before the court. Disjointed and confusing cross-examination may even irritate a judge and achieves nothing. The best cross-examination is sharp, pointed and brief. In my experience, even in complicated cases, it is possible to undertake effective cross-examination in less than an hour. Effective cross-examination keeps the Court interested from the first question to the last. As a general rule, the longer and meandering cross-examination the less effective it is.

Cross-examination of an expert witness

Cross-examination of expert witnesses, in my experience requires more skill and preparation. It seems to me that a lawyer must know as much as, or more than, the expert to be cross-examined upon a particular subject if such questioning is to be effective. These experts may be accountants, engineers, geologists, or other persons having knowledge of a specialized character. A lawyer cross-examining an expert witness must read as much as practically possible about the area of expertise of the witness and at the very least familiarize himself with the concepts.

A lawyer should know when to stop cross-examination. Quite often you have a very bad witness in

Court who is not cohesive or clear in anything he testifies about. It is often tempting to keep asking the witness a barrage of questions with the hope that he would eventually make sense. However, experience teaches that such witnesses are high risk and if a lawyer does not know when to stop, the witness may shock the lawyer with something that damages his case.

The Lawyer must be in control

The whole idea behind cross-examination is that the lawyer should be in control and force the witness to answer questions harmful to an opponent's case. When you ask an open ended question, or a question you do not know what the answer is likely to be you may regret why you asked that question and at that stage the harm may have already been done.

Credibility

Destroying the credibility of a witness is one of the most important functions of cross-examination. There are many ways of destroying the credibility of a witness without necessarily being rude or abusive. An effective cross-examination must seek to test, challenge and contest the witness's ability to remember or perceive the events. A lawyer must tread with care where he is confronted with a seemingly honest witness who has no axe to grind, and may have damaging evidence to present to the court. In such a situation, it may be safer to challenge his ability to perceive. For instance, in a claim involving a motor vehicle accident, it may be more rewarding and productive to challenge the witness's poor eye sight to the extent that that may be material.

It may also be useful to attack reliability. In the case of a car accident as indicated above, the ability of a witness to remember events correctly, although appearing far-fetched initially, may cumulatively considered suggest that the witness may not be trusted. For instance, a witness who previously made mistakes regarding dates, times, and places may be attempting to tell the truth, but there is a question as to whether the witness can accurately testify to events. In this particular instance, the purpose of cross-examination would not be to show the witness is lying but that the witness cannot be counted upon to testify accurately to what occurred.

Having regard to the above, a lawyer may want to ask a number of seemingly insignificant questions, which, considered in isolation may appear meaningless but considered cumulatively may assist his case a lot. For instance, you can show that the witness got some facts wrong, such as the colour of the vehicle. He may have been wrong about the date of the accident. He didn't accurately describe the model of the car. He testifies there were five (5) people in plaintiff's car when there were only three (3) people in it. None of these mistakes has anything to do with whether plaintiff drove at a speed that was excessive in the circumstances, but may cause a court to question whether this witness can present reliable testimony.

Often, the most effective attack on a witness is an attack on the witness's truthfulness. Where a witness is a proven liar, then in all likelihood the case he was called to support is likely to fail. Courts are unforgiving of witnesses they find not to be truthful. All that courts want is the truth to be told.

The most effective attacks on truthfulness or the absence thereof comes from showing that a witness has lied under oath. Thus, where testimony at trial is contradictory to testimony given soon after the event, say, an accident, and the testimony at the trial contradicts the evidence that the witness gave to the police soon after the accident took place, then the court may be unwilling to believe the witnesses' trial testimony. Where it is intended to attack the witnesses' truthfulness, it is important to focus on points directly related to the key issues in the case. Focussing on minor points to prove the witness is not truthful is ineffective and counter-productive.

An important rule

The rule in *Brown v Dunn* (1894(6) R67) is very important in cross-examination. It allows a party to know before closing their case what parts of his case is going to be challenged by evidence from a defence or adverse witness. The rule simply says the opposing party must put across his version of events. For instance if his defence that he intended to put forward involves a denial or contradiction of evidence given by another party, say the plaintiff's witness, then the defence version of facts should be put to the witness in cross-examination.

If a party ignores the aforesaid rule and later attempts to lead evidence that is inconsistent with the evidence led by rival witness, the court may exercise its discretion to disallow this evidence or take into account the failure to examine on the point when considering evidence at the end of a trial.

Conclusion

Effective cross-examination is the keystone of a successful trial. It can, and does make a difference between winning and losing a trial. The best cross-examination is a result of hard work and thorough preparation. It requires a well thought out plan and an excellent execution. It requires a thorough appreciation of what cross-examination is intended to achieve. It requires the ability to forego questioning a witness if that is not necessary.

CHAPTER SEVENTEEN

LAWYER'S FEES

Lawyers charge fees for their services. Lawyer's fees are generally expensive compared to other professions. A fee that is charged or the applicable rates must be disclosed to the clients. Clients should not be taken by surprise or otherwise ambushed with respect to how much they need to pay. The fees that are charged must be reasonable and in accordance with the applicable tariffs, if any.

A lawyers' bill is subject to be reviewed by an appropriate officer of the court, often called the Taxing Master. The Taxing Master or the designated officer has an obligation and mandate to ensure that the fees that are charged to clients reasonable and justifiable.

Costs are generally ordered by the court at its discretion. Generally a losing party pays the costs of the winner. It is common for lawyers to agree on reasonable costs. However, if no agreement is reached the taxing officer would determine the costs to be paid.

Withdrawals

A lawyer who has not been adequately paid may withdraw from a matter as a consequence. However, rules of court that prescribe such withdrawals must be complied with. Generally it is important not to withdraw at short notice.

The client must be allowed sufficient time to find a replacement.

It would be unethical for a lawyer to generate unnecessary postponements or voluminous pleadings or heads of arguments in order to justify an exorbitant fee that would otherwise not be due. Lawyers' fees are often taxable by a designated officer of the court who ensures that the fees levied against a client are justifiable and within the ambit of the applicable tariffs. In certain situations it is possible to contest the determination of a lawyer's bill by the taxing officer.

No win fee

In most commonwealth jurisdictions it is unacceptable to agree on a "no win no fee" arrangement. There appears to be flexibility on lawyers charging below the minimum allowed by the lawyer's tariffs.

High fees

Lawyers must provide their clients with the basis for charges and should desist from charging high fees. In certain jurisdictions, such as Botswana, where tariffs have been determined and set in the rules of the High Court, fees charged to the client must be in terms thereof. In the absence of such determined and set fees, it is legitimate to consider the following when charging a client:

- ☐ The time required;
- ☐ The novelty and difficulty of the questions involved;

- The urgency of the matter; and
- The experience, reputation and ability of the lawyer.

It is generally understood that since urgent matters may well take a lawyer from other deserving business and focus his mind and time on a matter that cannot wait, it is permissible to charge fees that are be higher than doing a matter in the ordinary course.

Conclusion

It is important that lawyers charge reasonable and justifiable fees. This means that fees must reflect the nature and complexity of the lawyer's tasks. Lawyers must keep within the set tariffs, where applicable and must inform clients about the costs of their professional services. At the end of the day it seems only ethical that a lawyer should try as much as possible to achieve the most cost effective resolution of the client's matter.

CHAPTER EIGHTEEN

DISCIPLINE

In most jurisdictions the law governing the practice of law makes provisions for the discipline of lawyers for misconduct. The law typically makes provision for what constitutes misconduct and how any disciplinary process arising from a charge of misconduct may be handled.

Law societies

Law societies are the professional bodies that are often established to ensure that lawyers perform their duties professionally. Being professional requires that lawyers be properly qualified and subscribe to set standards that govern the practice of law.

The public must be able to have confidence in the legal profession and the administration of justice. To this end it is desirable that clearly articulated rules of conduct are introduced – not only so that the profession is aware of their ethical obligations but also because it is in public interest to do so.

Over commercialization

Of recent concern has been expressed over commercialization of law and the subordination of service and professionalism to profit, personal aims and ambitions. This distracts against the honourable nature of the profession.

Disciplinary proceedings against lawyers should be brought before an impartial disciplinary committee established by the legal profession or before an independent statutory authority or before a court. In Botswana, by way of example, the task of conducting disciplinary proceedings against errant lawyers is vested in the disciplinary committee of the law society. These proceedings, if brought, are often subject to an independent judicial review.

In most jurisdictions, courts may on their own motion refer a lawyer to a professional body of which he is a member for breach of a professional code of conduct. This is because these bodies are responsible to ensure that their members conduct themselves appropriately.

Sanctions

A lawyer who is found to have breached the professional code of conduct may be sanctioned as appropriate, such as being warned, reprimanded, suspended, fined or a revocation of the license to practice law.

There are a number of possible breaches that range from minor to serious. These may include:

a) Insulting colleagues and judges performing professional functions;

b) Refusing to provide back the files to former clients despite the fact that the client has paid the lawyer requisite fees;

c) Acting contrary to the provisions of the law;

d) Over charging or of reaching a client;

e) Revealing a client secrets thereby breaching the rule of lawyer/client privilege;

f) Misappropriation client's funds.

Conclusion

Lawyers should always be disciplined, and ensure that their conduct is beyond reproach. They should not engage in any conduct that may bring the legal profession, and indeed the administration of justice into disrepute. They should not allow their personal preferences or emotions to override their fidelity to the law. In most jurisdictions professional associations are there to ensure that lawyers abide by their professional ethics.

Exercising discipline requires adherence to professional ethical obligations, diligence, professional skill, commitment to the law and more broadly to ensuring the rule of law and efficient and effective administration of justice.

CHAPTER NINETEEN
CONCLUSION

One of the key messages of this publication is that the legal profession can only work to regain public confidence, which it seems to be losing, if they go back to basics and honour the ethics and etiquette that define this noble and honourable profession.

Public expectations

My brother and friend Justice Kirby, former Judge of the High Court in Australia, now retired, once wrote that the public appears to have large expectations of lawyers but a diminishing estimation of the likelihood that they will be fulfilled. All members of the legal fraternity must be seriously concerned by this observation.

Members of the public are correctly concerned of lawyers turning up in court late, dragging their feet to complete their matters in court, overcharging and other unbecoming conduct. Members of the public across many jurisdictions feel that some lawyers lack integrity and honesty and that the law is failing to deliver just results to the community.

Traditions and conventions

An ethical legal profession steeped in traditions and conventions of the law is a prerequisite to an effective justice system that is trusted by the people. Ethics act as an important guide to ensure proper conduct from lawyers. Law is a profession and lawyers have obligations to their clients and to the courts. They often say ethics is the heart and soul of the profession. Well- functioning justice systems are important for the sustenance of the rule of law and maintenance of order and stability. It is for these reason that all of us involved in the justice system must recommit to an ethical practice of law characterized by civility, courtesy, integrity and professionalism. Reclaiming ethical standards of the profession should be a top priority for any jurisdiction. Ethical practice of law should also be a priority for the courts and law curriculum of any country.

As indicated in the introductory chapter the reality in most jurisdictions across the Commonwealth is that ethical standards are on the decline. This should concern the entire legal fraternity and members of the public. Self- evidently many lawyers in most jurisdictions are increasingly paying less heed to rules of professional conduct and etiquette. It is also important that law schools should step in to fill the gap by strengthening teaching of legal ethics as that is foundational to the professional life of a lawyer.

Legal education

It is my considered view that cultivation of the highest ethical standards and etiquette begins with a lawyer's education, often at law schools, and his early practical training, during pupillage. It continues throughout his life at law, learning and continuously upgrading himself in the form of continuing legal education.

At law schools, at least at the University of Botswana, where I completed my law degree, and subsequently taught law, the legal ethics curriculum at the time seemed, with benefit of hindsight, to be deficient, at least in so far as it provided, then, very limited, if any, interaction of the students with the courts and the legal profession.

At its most comprehensive level ethical practice of law must be part of continuous legal education. This involves a holistic approach to improving ethical standards amongst lawyers involving courts, which manifests or translates into high quality legal practice.

Measurement

The above objective may only be achieved if, the law societies in particular, put in place some mechanism in which they could measure and or monitor the extent to which lawyers comply with ethical standards.

I emphasise measurement and monitoring because experience with respect to anything that needs to be done, shows that no tangible results can accrue to anything without measurement.

It is therefore absolutely important that the courts and the law societies should forge a strong professional relationship to raise and monitor high standards in the legal profession. This means that whenever the courts raise some issues to be investigated by law societies; that must be done without fail because courts would not lightly raise such issues unless they deserve further investigation.

The ethical education for lawyers must concern all the players in the legal system. It must start at law schools, where lawyers must be thoroughly grounded in legal ethics and etiquette.

Fidelity to the law

In the course of legal practice, the judges or the legal system as a whole must develop keen interest in further cultivating fidelity to ethical behaviour and their duty to uphold the rule of law. The duty to uphold the rule of law requires that lawyers should uphold and observe the rule of law, provide and foster the cause of justice and maintain high professional standards and not to engage in any conduct that is unbecoming of a lawyer. There is no doubt in my mind that the whole purpose of the rule that enjoins lawyers to uphold the rule of law was to ensure that the legal profession is seen as a noble profession that is an effective watchdog of the people's interests.

For completeness, it seems in order to summarise the important highlights, canvassed, in this book, for convenience, as follows:

Good behaviour

Good behaviour towards the judges, other lawyers and court users generally is very important. Any misbehaviour or ill-manners may alienate the counsel from court staff and, even worse, the judge. It therefore makes sense to be careful not to antagonize these categories of people in the course of performing their duties.

Tardiness

Tardiness is the habit of being late. Walking into a courtroom after a session is over is evidence of tardiness. Some lawyers are in the habit of late coming, filing deficient papers or otherwise improperly dressed. Tardiness is a breach of a lawyers duty to the courts, because among other things, it causes delay and disrupts court process. Lawyers must take time management seriously. Quite often people who are late are considered disorganised, disrespectful, selfish or even looking for attention. In some cases tardiness may amount to contempt of court. Lawyers who come to court late risk not being heard. In some cases judges refuse to hear lawyers who come to court late.

Incivility

The duty of civility owed to a fellow lawyer is akin to respect and reverence which in a sign of maturity, competence and self-control. In the legal profession, it is given that any lawyer who employs any rash, uncouth approach to a fellow lawyer in court or in their interaction, does more harm to his personal integrity. Civility is about courtesy to other human beings. Judges would invariably give you the opportunity to speak if you do so respectfully. Rudeness and discourtesy does not advance a lawyer's arguments.

Lack of Brevity

Brevity is a virtue in legal practice. Catch the judge's attention immediately at the beginning of your submissions. As I always say to lawyers: put your best foot forward at the earliest opportunity. A disjointed and long winded argument is frequently a losing argument. A succinct and crisp argument captures the judge's notice and has a better chance of being successful.

In drafting papers a lawyer must aim for brevity and clarity. If you bury the legal issue within a mountain of extraneous hostile verbiage, then you unwittingly bury your case. No judge likes wading through voluminous files to unearth a simple but critical fact, such as the speed at which the defendant driver was driving, if the negligence suit is based on driving at a speed that was excessive.

Casualness

Court decorum is absolutely important in the orderly dispatch of court business. A courtroom is not a place to chat with your friends, to text, whisper or giggle. It is unbecoming for lawyers to whisper, giggle or nod their heads in disapproval or approval of anything said in court.

Counsels should address each other by their last name rather than a more casual appellation. In court and on the record, counsel should refer to opposing counsel as my learned friend, or Mr. Dingake. It is also not proper for a lawyer to address a question directly to the opposing counsel while on the record. The appropriate procedure is to request the judge to pose the inquiry to opposing counsel about an issue.

Addressing the Court

Lawyers must exhibit due respect to the court. When you address the court, look directly at the judge, even if your message is to be acted upon by another member of the court. Remember court is not necessarily the person of the judge, but, an organ of the State, that wields judicial power.

When someone is addressing the court, when he has the floor, he is entitled to be fully and fairly heard. Members of the audience, including lawyers, should listen to court proceedings in total silence. It is discourteous to talk in court when the court is in session. Lawyers should admonish their clients and witnesses to never show any outward response to anything said or done in the courtroom. If the opposition is lying through its teeth, there is no need to be disruptive as the court would always allow all parties an opportunity to say their side of the story.

When addressing the court, counsel should avoid saying something like, "The court's attention is directed to…" or "The court will note…". If you want the court to take notice of something, it is advisable to preface your presentation with, "The court's attention is invited…" or "May it please the court…" It is not appropriate to say to the judge, "Your attention is invited," because you are addressing the court through the judge, you are not addressing the judge himself. "Your lordship, the court's attention is invited…," because the phrase "Your lordship" serves only to open the channel of communication.

Dress

Dress code for lawyers is laden with meaning. Your appearance broadcasts your attitude. You can be certain that if you are dressed shabbily you are likely not to be taken seriously. It is true that a shabbily dressed lawyer technically short changes himself on his right of audience in that there is a strong likelihood that the psychology of the court may be repulsive to the submission of such counsel.

Relations out of Court

Interactions of lawyers must always be friendly. There is no need for personal hostility. Your case is in court, and that's where the 'fight' will be conducted according to the rules. It is important how you conduct your 'battle'. Do it with friendliness and courtesy. Even if your enemy would not hesitate to stab you in the back, as it often happens, remain civil and friendly. Rather let your opponent be the one who appears an 'uncultured professional'.

Lawyers must also be civil and courteous to court staff. The Registry staff plays a pivotal role as they are the ones that receipt court papers. If the court clerk refuses to file your papers because of some incorrectly perceived error, then do it his way as long as you suffer no significant loss of rights.

Don't be too eager to take advantage of insignificant mistakes. Remember, the opposition is human too. They are bound to make mistakes. There are certain mistakes that are explainable and harmless. Yes, some mistakes may be costly. Don't be too quick to take advantage of an opponent's mistake that may cast you in bad light. Always be fair and friendly.

Humility

Humility is essential to legal craft. Lawyers, even most experienced ones, do not necessarily know it all. Lawyers should admit the things they do not know, and be prepared to learn at all times. It is perfectly in order to concede a weak point. Lawyers should be prepared to learn, and to accept to be corrected where they go wrong.

Avoid Corrupt Practice

Corruption is rife in some countries. Litigants often attempt to bribe court staff and even judges. Recently, (2020) a judge in Malawi reported attempts to bribe him. No lawyer should be involved in acts of corruption.

Conclusion

Etiquette lies at the heart of the nobility of the legal profession, and is accomplished through the control of entry into the profession.

Law is a profession and lawyers have certain ethical obligations to comply with. These obligations are generally articulated in the rules of professional conduct. We must do everything possible to keep the legal profession a noble one and ensure that the public respects the profession and its members. As it is often said to whom much is given, so much is also expected.

REFERENCES

1. Alli v Ayinde, (2010) ALL FWLR PT540 @ Pag 1333.

2. Bagaric M, 'In Defence of a Utilitarian Theory of Punishment: Punishing the Innocent the Compatibility of Utilitarianism and Rights' (1999) 24 *Australian Journal of Legal Philosophy 95,* (2000), ch 4.

3. Barry J, "The Ethics of Advocacy' (1941) 15 *Australian Law Journal* 166, 168.

4. Basten J, "Control and the Lawyer-Client Relationship' (1981) 6 *Journal of the Legal Profession* 7, 34.

5. Boulton W, *A Guide to Conduct and Etiquette at the Bar* (Butterworths, 6th ed, 1975) 70-72.

6. Cain J and Hammond K, 'Tending the Bar: Lawyers are expected to Act Ethically. Whose Job is to ensure they do?", *The Age* (Melbourne), 18 August 2002, 16.

7. Campbell T, *The Legal Theory of Ethical Positivism* (Dartmouth Publishing, 1996) 161-88.

8. Code of Conduct of the Bar of England.

9. Dal Pont G, *Lawyers' Professional Responsibility* (LBC Information Services, 1996) 14.

10. Disney J et at, *Lawyers* (Law Book Company, 2nd ed, 1986) 597-8.

11. Eleko v Baddeley, (1925) 6 NLR 65 at 68.

12. Faine J, 'What is happening to our Profession?' (1997) *Australian Lawyer* 40.

13. Fife-Yeomans J, 'Lawyers Do it For Love, Not Money', *The Weekend Australian*, 16-17 August 1997, 11.

14. Freeman S, 'Contractualism, Moral Motivation & Practical Reason' (1987) 88 *Journal of Philosophy* 281 – 304.

15. Freedmann M, *Lawyers' Ethics in an Adversary System* (Bobbs-Merrill, 1975) 10.

16. Galanter M and Palay T, 'Large Law Firms and Professional Responsibility' in R Cranston (ed), *Legal Ethics and Professional Responsibility* (oxford University Press, 1995) 198.

17. Hart L A H, *Essays in Jurisprudence and Philosophy* (Clarendon Press, 1983), 196-7.

18. Hart L A H, 'Bentham on Legal Rights' in A W B Simpson (ed) *Oxford Essays in Jurisprudence* (Clarendon Press, 2nd ed, 1973) 171.

19. *International Code of Ethics* (International Bar Association).

20. Kwaptoe v Tsenyil, (1999) 4 NWLR (PT 600) 571 at 574 F-G.

21. Linowitz S with Mayer M, *The Betrayed Profession: Lawyering at the end of the Twentieth Century* (Charles Scribner's Sons, 1994) 25-26.

22. Luban D, 'Introduction: A new Canadian Legal Ethics' (1996) 1 *Canadian Journal of Law and Jurisprudence* 1.

23. New South Wales Law Reform Commission, *First Report on the Legal Profession* (1982) [6], 78.

24. Nwanko v Onongze-Madu, (2009) 1 NWLR (pt 1123) @ 671 at 714 parg A-D.

25. Obi v Dr Chris Ngige, (2012) 1 NWLR Pt.1280, 1 @ 32-33.

26. O'Dair R, in *Legal Ethics: Text and Materials* (Butterworths, 2001) 17.

27. Rizzo P, 'Morals for Home, Morals for Office. The Double Ethical Life of a Civil Litigator' (1993) *Catholic Lawyer* 89.

28. Rondel v Worsley, 1969, AC 191 at 227.

29. Ross S and McFarlane P, *Lawyers' Responsibility and Accountability* (Butterworths, 1997) 192.

30. Satris S, *Taking Sides: Clashing Views on Controversial Moral issues* (Duskin Publishing, 1988).

31. Shiel F, 'Push for ethics Advisers at Law Firms', *The Age* (Melbourne), 6 September 2002, 7

32. Schwartz M, *Lawyers and the Legal Profession* (Bobbs-Merrill Company, 2nd ed, 1985) 49.

Made in United States
Orlando, FL
09 July 2024